Thought and Language

L. S. Vygotsky

Edited and translated by
Eugenia Hanfmann and Gertrude Vakar

THE M. I. T. PRESS
Massachusetts Institute of Technology
Cambridge, Massachusetts

Introduction

Jerome S. Bruner

LEV SEMENOVICH VYGOTSKY was born in 1896. In his student days at the University of Moscow he read widely and avidly in the fields of linguistics, social science, psychology, philosophy, and the arts. His systematic work in psychology did not begin until 1924. Ten years later he died of tuberculosis at the age of 38. In that period, with the collaboration of such able students and co-workers as Luria, Leontiev, and Sakharov, he launched a series of investigations in developmental psychology, education, and psychopathology, many of which were interrupted by his untimely death. The present volume, published posthumously in 1934, ties together one major phase of Vygotsky's work, and though its principal theme is the relation of thought and language, it is more deeply a presentation of a highly original and thoughtful theory of intellectual development. Vygotsky's conception of development is at the same time a theory of education.

For an English-speaking audience, it avails little to trace the ideological course of Vygotsky's work through the groundswells and storms of psychology in the Soviet Union. It was inevitable that his work should disturb the doctrinaire guardians of "proper Marxian interpretation," particularly during the period of the "battle for consciousness." As two of Vygotsky's most gifted collaborators, Luria and Leontiev, put it in 1958, introducing German translations of his work in the *Zeitschrift für Psychologie,* "The first and most important task of that time [the late 1920's and 1930's when the 'battle for consciousness' raged] consisted of freeing oneself, on the one hand, from vulgar behaviorism, and, on the other, from the subjective approach to mental phenomena as exclusively inner subjective conditions which can only be investigated introspectively." It is no surprise then that Vygotsky's *Thought and Language* should have been suppressed in 1936, two years after its appearance, not to reappear again until 1956. For he would not brook either materialist reductionism or mentalism, nor the easy Cartesian dualism that opted frontally for one and let the other in through the back door. Indeed, at the very beginning of his career as a psychologist, Vygotsky wrote: "In that psychology ignores the problem of consciousness, it blocks itself off from access to the investigation of complicated problems of human behavior, and the elimination of consciousness from the sphere of scientific psychology has as its major consequence the retention of all the dualism and spiritualism of earlier subjective psychology." Though the book was officially suppressed, it continued to have a major impact upon the thinking of a generation of Russian psychologists, linguists, and psychopathologists.

In terms of our own intellectual perspective, Vygotsky's views can be labeled superficially as functionalism or instrumentalism, or possibly as like Act Psychology. From the Marxist ideological perspective, he is celebrated as the man who recognized the historical determination of man's consciousness and intellect. But looking at Vygotsky's place in world psychology, his position transcends either the usual functionalism of the Dewey-James variety or the conventional historical materialism of Marxist ideology. Vygotsky is an original. It is a disservice to him either to find his significance solely in developing Soviet conceptions of man or to render him by gloss translation into the language of functionalism or to see only his kinship to George Herbert Mead, to whom he has an interesting resemblance.

You will find this epigraph at the head of one of Vygotsky's books, *"Natura parendo vincitur,"* and indeed *Thought and Language* elaborates in what sense he believed that in mastering nature we master ourselves. For it is the internalization of overt action that makes thought, and particularly the internalization of external dialogue that brings the powerful tool of language to bear on the stream of thought. Man, if you will, is shaped by the tools and instruments that he comes to use, and neither the mind nor the hand alone can amount to much. Vygotsky follows the epigraph above with a quotation from Bacon: *"Nec manus, nisi intellectus, sibi permissus, multam valent: instrumentis et auxilibus res perficitur."* And if neither hand nor intellect alone prevails, the tools and aids that do are the developing streams of internalized language and conceptual thought that sometimes run parallel and sometimes merge, each affecting the other.

Vygotsky's thought is presented so clearly in this translation that there is little need in this preface to render his theory and work in summary. He places his view about the relation of language and thought in the perspective of theories of the phylogeny of intellectual development with particularly detailed attention given to the earlier work of Koehler and Yerkes on the great apes. His position is very much in accord with the more modern work of physical anthropologists who have speculated on the use of hand "pebble tools" in shaping the evolution of *Australopithecus* and other hominids. Indeed, had Vygotsky been an anatomist, he most surely would have aligned himself with the view, so dear to William James, that function creates organ. Having concluded that speech and thought come from different roots and that the close correspondence between thought and speech that is found in man is not present in higher anthropoids, he plunges directly into the task of exploring the behavior of young children where there is a prelinguistic phase in the use of thought and a preintellectual phase in the use of speech. Three writers on the development of thought and speech serve him as points of departure: Karl Buehler, William Stern, and Jean Piaget. Of Piaget, Vygotsky knew only his first two books. In a separately published pamphlet,* Piaget relates his development since the early 1930's to Vygotsky's work, with which he was not acquainted in detail until the present translation was made available to him.

In dealing with intellectual and linguistic development in

* Jean Piaget, *Comments on Vygotsky's Critical Remarks,* Cambridge, The M.I.T. Press, 1962.

children, Vygotsky develops his theme concerning the internalization of dialogue into inner speech and thought, contrasting his view with the then point of view of Piaget on speech development as the suppression of egocentrism, and providing both psychology and linguistics with the deepest analysis of inner speech. He dismisses the crass position of Watson that equates thought with faint muscular activity and makes clear that, unlike Max, he does not see internalized speech as muscular tremors in the larynx but as internal representation. The treatment is analytic and theoretical in the best sense. Systematic experimentation is scarce, but where experiment and observation are reported, they are of such an ingenuity that one wishes there had been more — like the observation on children describing a picture in words as compared to acting out what the picture is about.

It is when Vygotsky comes to the discussion of the development of conceptual grouping in children — from heaps to complexes to pseudo-concepts to true concepts — that one recognizes his power and ingenuity as an empiricist. Using the Vygotsky blocks, perhaps the only thing for which the author had been known in this country, he traces the manner in which the intellectual development of the child is given a classificatory structure that makes possible the use of language as a logical and analytic tool in thinking. Before that, in the absence of conceptual structures, language plays other roles, but not this one. Finally, Vygotsky explores the manner in which the more rigorous concepts of science and disciplined thought have the effect of transforming and giving new direction to the growth of "spontaneous" concepts in children. I leave to the reader the delight of discovering Vygotsky's conception of intelligence as a capacity to benefit from instruction and his radical proposal that we test intelligence accordingly.

The book is, in many ways, more programmatic than systematic. It is at times distressingly swift in coming to conclusions that are reasonable in that special twilight shed by common-sense observation. But even then, the common sense Vygotsky brings to his task is not from the armchair but from incessant observation of children learning to talk and learning to solve problems. Vygotsky's untimely death cut off a developing stream of experiments; yet his work is only now beginning to be reflected in the vigorous activity of contemporary Soviet psychologists and linguists.

Only one further point need be made in introducing this powerful and original book. Vygotsky represents still another step forward in the growing effort to understand cognitive processes. His is a mediational point of view. Concepts and the language that infuses and instruments them give power and strategy to cognitive activity. The capacity to impose superordinate structures in the interest of seeing things more simply and deeply is seen as one of the powerful tools of human intelligence. Take a comment at random. "The new higher concepts in turn transform the meaning of the lower. The adolescent who has mastered algebraic concepts has gained a vantage point from which he sees arithmetical concepts in a broader perspective." Throughout these pages there is repeated emphasis on man's capacity to create higher order structures that, in effect, replace and give new power to the conceptual structures that one climbed over en route to higher order mastery. It is an image of man that places the effort to learn and master into the center of the stage as an instrument that frees us of earlier efforts and results. "In this as in other instances of passing from one level of meaning to the next, the child does not have to restructure separately all of his earlier concepts, which indeed would be a Sisyphean labor. Once a new structure has been incorporated into his thinking . . . it gradually spreads to the older concepts as they are drawn into the intellectual operations of the higher type." Granted Vygotsky is stating a program of inquiry in such remarks rather than a tested conclusion; yet he is putting the issue in a form that carries with it a vigorous and intelligent image of man.

Vygotsky has indeed introduced an historical perspective into the understanding of how thought develops, and indeed what thought is. But what is interesting is that he has also proposed a mechanism whereby one becomes free of one's history. It is to

Vygotsky that Soviet psychologists turn in examining the manner in which man fights free from the dominance of stimulus-response conditioning of the classical Pavlovian type. Vygotsky is the architect of the Second Signal System, proposed by Pavlov in reaction against the excessive rigidity of his earlier theories. It is the Second Signal System that provides the means whereby man creates a mediator between himself and the world of physical stimulation so that he can react in terms of his own symbolic conception of reality. What pleases Marxist theorists in the conception is the clearly recognized role of society and social activity in giving shape to the Second Signal System — the mediating structures through which the stimulus signals of the physical world are filtered. To me, the striking fact is that given a pluralistic world where each comes to terms with the environment in his own style, Vygotsky's developmental theory is also a description of the many roads to individuality and freedom. It is in this sense, I think, that he transcends, as a theorist of the nature of man, the ideological rifts that divide our world so deeply today.

Cambridge, Massachusetts
July, 1961

Translators' Preface*

THE FIRST Russian edition of *Thought and Language*† appeared
a few months after the author's death. In preparing the book
for publication, Vygotsky attempted to combine separate essays
into a coherent whole. Several of them had been written earlier,
and some had been published; others were dictated during Vygotsky's last illness. Perhaps because the book was prepared in
haste, it is not very well organized and its essential inner unity
is not readily apparent. Some discussions are repeated almost
word for word in different chapters or even in the same chapter;
numerous polemical digressions obscure the development of
thought. The editor of the first Russian edition pointed out
some of these flaws in his preface but decided to leave Vygotsky's text intact. Twenty-two years later, when *Thought and
Language* was republished in a volume of Vygotsky's selected
works,‡ very few changes were made.

In the late thirties, one of the translators of the present edition, E. Hanfmann, in collaboration with J. Kasanin, repeated
some of Vygotsky's studies of concept formation; she remembers
vividly the struggle of winding her way through his text. When
Vygotsky's collaborator and friend Professor A. R. Luria approached her in 1957 with the request that she participate in the
translation of *Thought and Language,* she expressed her convic-
tion that a literal translation would not do justice to Vygotsky's

* The translation was supported by a Public Health Service research
grant, T-13, from the Division of General Medical Sciences, Public Health
Service.
† Soc.-econom. izd., Moscow-Leningrad, 1934.
‡ Izd. akad. pedag. nauk, Moscow, 1956.

thought. It was agreed that excessive repetition and certain polemical discussions that would be of little interest to the contemporary reader should be eliminated, in favor of a more straightforward exposition. In translating the book, we have simplified and clarified Vygotsky's involved style, while striving always to render his meaning exactly. The internal organization of the chapters has been preserved, except in Chapter 2, where extensive omissions resulted in a rearrangement of the text and in a greatly reduced number of subdivisions.

Although our more compact rendition could be called an abridged version of the original, we feel that the condensation has increased clarity and readability without any loss of thought content or factual information. Unfortunately, the Russian text contained no detailed information on Vygotsky's own and his co-workers' studies: of the four series of investigations referred to in the book, the method of only one, Shif's [37], was described in some detail. Several of the studies were briefly reported at congresses and in journals [47, 49], but, according to Professor Luria, none was published in full.

The bibliography of the Russian edition is reproduced at the end of the book, with some additions. In spite of these, the bibliography does not adequately reflect the range of the sources Vygotsky used. His treatment of references was very unsystematic. Some of the publications he included in the bibliographical list are not directly referred to in his text. On the other hand, many of the authors discussed in the text are not included in his list, nor does the list contain the many linguistic works with which the author was obviously familiar. We have corrected some of the omissions. For instance, we have included in the bibliography Ach's study of concept formation, which Vygotsky discusses in detail. Besides, we have added two articles by Vygotsky published in American periodicals [51, 52], as well as the two early reports on his work in English [15, 16] and a recent report in German [25]. The majority of the titles of German, French, and American works were given by Vygotsky in the original languages; some, however, were listed in their Russian translations; these we have replaced by the original titles.

All the quotations have been translated from the Russian as given by Vygotsky, including those from non-Russian authors with the exception of the numerous and often lengthy passages from Piaget, which we have translated directly from the French.

We are grateful to The Williams & Wilkins Company for permission to quote from *Conceptual Thinking in Schizophrenia,* by E. Hanfmann and J. Kasanin,* and to the editors of *Psychiatry* for permission to reprint an early translation of Chapter 7 by H. Beier.† We did utilize portions of her text, including the rendition of several quotations from Russian literary works; we had to retranslate the chapter in part, however, to achieve a uniform degree of condensation and a consistent style.

Last but not least, we are very grateful to Professor Jean Piaget for his comments on Vygotsky's critique of his early work.

E. HANFMANN

G. VAKAR

* *Nerv. and Ment. Dis. Monogr.,* 67, 1942.
† L. S. Vygotsky, "Thought and Speech," *Psychiatry* II, 1, 1939.

Contents

Thought and Language

Author's Preface

THIS BOOK is a study of one of the most complex problems of psychology, the interrelation of thought and language. As far as we know, it has not yet been investigated experimentally in a systematic fashion. We have attempted at least a first approach to this task by conducting experimental studies of a number of separate aspects of the total problem. The results provide a part of the material on which our analyses are based.

Theoretical and critical discussions are a necessary precondition and a complement of the experimental part of the study and constitute a large portion of our book. The working hypotheses that serve as starting points for our fact-finding experiments had to be based on a general theory of the genetic roots of thought and language. In order to develop such a theoretical framework, we reviewed and carefully analyzed the pertinent data in psychological literature. Concomitantly, we subjected to critical analysis the leading theories of thought and language in the hope of overcoming their insufficiencies and avoiding their pitfalls in our own search for the theoretical path to follow.

Inevitably, our analysis encroached on some neighboring fields, such as linguistics and the psychology of education. In discussing the development of scientific concepts in childhood, we made use of the working hypothesis concerning the relation between the educational process and mental development, which we had evolved elsewhere using a different body of data.

The structure of this book is perforce complex and multi-faceted, yet all its parts are oriented toward a central task, the genetic analysis of the relationship between thought and the spoken word. Chapter 1 poses the problem and discusses the method. Chapters 2 and 3 are critical analyses of the two most influential theories about the development of language and thinking, Piaget's and Stern's. Chapter 4 attempts to trace the genetic roots of thought and language; it serves as a theoretical introduction to the main part of the book, the two experimental investigations described in the next two chapters. The first study (Chapter 5) deals with the general developmental course of word meanings in childhood; the second (Chapter 6) is a comparative study of the development of the "scientific" and the spontaneous concepts of the child. The last chapter attempts to draw together the threads of our investigations and to present the total process of verbal thought as it appears in the light of our data.

It may be useful to enumerate briefly the aspects of our work that we believe to be novel and consequently in need of further careful checking. Apart from our modified formulation of the problem and the partially new method, our contribution may be summarized as follows: (1) providing experimental evidence that meanings of words undergo evolution during childhood, and defining the basic steps in that evolution; (2) uncovering the singular way in which the child's "scientific" concepts develop, compared with his spontaneous concepts, and formulating the laws governing their development; (3) demonstrating the specific psychological nature and linguistic function of written speech in its relation to thinking; and (4) clarifying, by way of experiments, the nature of inner speech and its relation to thought. The evaluation of our findings and of the interpretations we have given them is hardly the author's province and must be left to our readers and critics.

The author and his associates have been exploring the field of language and thought for almost ten years, in the course of which some of the initial hypotheses were revised, or abandoned as false. The main line of our investigation, however, has followed the direction taken from the start. We fully realize the inevitable imperfections of this study, which is no more than a first step in a new direction. Yet we feel that in uncovering the problem of thought and language as the focal issue of human psychology we have contributed to some essential progress. Our findings point the way to a new theory of consciousness, which is barely touched upon at the end of our book.

1

The Problem and the Approach

THE STUDY of thought and language is one of the areas of psychology in which a clear understanding of interfunctional relations is particularly important. As long as we do not understand the interrelation of thought and word, we cannot answer, or even correctly pose, any of the more specific questions in this area. Strange as it may seem, psychology has never investigated the relationship systematically and in detail. Interfunctional relations in general have not as yet received the attention they merit. The atomistic and functional modes of analysis prevalent during the past decade treated psychic processes in isolation. Methods of research were developed and perfected with a view to studying separate functions, while their interdependence and their organization in the structure of consciousness as a whole remained outside the field of investigation.

The unity of consciousness and the interrelation of all psychological functions were, it is true, accepted by all; the single functions were assumed to operate inseparably, in an uninterrupted connection with one another. But in the old psychology the unchallengeable premise of unity was combined with a set of tacit assumptions that nullified it for all practical purposes. It was taken for granted that the relation between two given functions never varied; that perception, for example, was always connected in an identical way with attention, memory with perception, thought with memory. As constants, these relationships could be, and were, factored out and ignored in the study of the separate functions. Because the relationships remained in fact inconsequential, the development of consciousness was seen as determined by the autonomous development of the single functions. Yet all that is known about psychic development indicates that its very essence lies in the change of the interfunctional structure of consciousness. Psychology must make these relations and their developmental changes the main problem, the focus of study, instead of merely postulating the general interrelation of all functions. This shift in approach is imperative for the productive study of language and thought.

A look at the results of former investigations of thought and language will show that all the theories offered from antiquity to our time range between *identification,* or *fusion,* of thought and speech on the one hand, and their equally absolute, almost metaphysical *disjunction* and *segregation* on the other. Whether expressing one of these extremes in pure form or combining them, that is, taking an intermediate position but always somewhere along the axis between the two poles, all the various theories on thought and language stay within the confining circle.

We can trace the idea of identity of thought and speech from the speculation of psychological linguistics that thought is "speech minus sound" to the theories of modern American psychologists and reflexologists who consider thought a reflex inhibited in its motor part. In all these theories the question of the relationship between thought and speech loses meaning. If they are one and the same thing, no relationship between them can arise. Those who identify thought with speech simply close the door on the problem. At first glance, the adherents of the opposite view seem to be in a better position. In regarding speech as the outward manifestation, the mere vestment, of thought, and in trying (as does the Wuerzburg school) to free thought from all sensory components including words, they not only pose but in their own way attempt to solve the problem of the relationship between the two functions.

Actually, however, they are unable to pose it in a manner that would permit a real solution. Having made thought and speech independent and "pure," and having studied each apart from the other, they are forced to see the relationship between them merely as a mechanical, external connection between two distinct processes. The analysis of verbal thinking into two separate, basically different elements precludes any study of the intrinsic relations between language and thought.

The fault thus lies in the *methods of analysis* adopted by previous investigators. To cope successfully with the problem of the relationship between thought and language, we must ask ourselves first of all what method of analysis is most likely to ensure its solution.

Two essentially different modes of analysis are possible in the study of psychological structures. It seems to us that one of them is responsible for all the failures that have beset former investigators of the old problem, which we are about to tackle in our turn, and that the other is the only correct way to approach it.

The first method analyzes complex psychological wholes into *elements*. It may be compared to the chemical analysis of water into hydrogen and oxygen, neither of which possesses the properties of the whole and each of which possesses properties not present in the whole. The student applying this method in looking for the explanation of some property of water — why it extinguishes fire, for example — will find to his surprise that hydrogen burns and oxygen sustains fire. These discoveries will not help him much in solving the problem. Psychology winds up in the same kind of dead end when it analyzes verbal thought into its components, thought and word, and studies them in isolation from each other. In the course of analysis, the original properties of verbal thought have disappeared. Nothing is left to the investigator but to search out the mechanical interaction of the two elements in the hope of reconstructing, in a purely speculative way, the vanished properties of the whole.

This type of analysis shifts the issue to a level of greater generality; it provides no adequate basis for the study of the multiform concrete relations between thought and language that arise in the course of the development and functioning of verbal thought in its various aspects. Instead of enabling us to examine and explain specific instances and phases, and to determine concrete regularities in the course of events, this method produces generalities pertaining to all speech and all thought. It leads us, moreover, into serious errors by ignoring the unitary nature of the process under study. The living union of sound and meaning that we call word is broken up into two parts, which are assumed to be held together merely by mechanical associative connections.

The view that sound and meaning in words are separate elements leading separate lives has done much harm to the study of both the phonetic and the semantic aspects of language. The most thorough study of speech sounds merely as sounds, apart from their connection with thought, has little bearing on their function as human speech since it does not bring out the physical and psychological properties peculiar to speech but only the properties common to all sounds existing in nature. In the same way, meaning divorced from speech sounds can only be studied as a pure act of thought, changing and developing independently of its material vehicle. This separation of sound and meaning is largely responsible for the barrenness of classical phonetics and semantics. In child psychology, likewise, the phonetic and the semantic aspects of speech development have been studied separately. The phonetic development has been studied in great detail, yet all the accumulated data contribute little to our understanding of linguistic development as such and remain essentially unrelated to the findings concerning the development of thinking.

In our opinion the right course to follow is to use the other type of analysis, which may be called *analysis into units.*

By *unit* we mean a product of analysis which, unlike elements, retains all the basic properties of the whole and which cannot be further divided without losing them. Not the chemical composition of water but its molecules and their behavior are the key to the understanding of the properties of water. The true unit of biological analysis is the living cell, possessing the basic properties of the living organism.

What is the unit of verbal thought that meets these requirements? We believe that it can be found in the internal aspect of the word, in *word meaning*. Few investigations of this internal aspect of speech have been undertaken so far, and psychology can tell us little about word meaning that would not apply in equal measure to all other images and acts of thought. The nature of meaning as such is not clear. Yet it is in word meaning that thought and speech unite into verbal thought. In meaning, then, the answers to our questions about the relationship between thought and speech can be found.

Our experimental investigation, as well as theoretical analysis, suggest that both Gestalt and association psychology have been looking for the intrinsic nature of word meaning in the wrong directions. A word does not refer to a single object but to a group or to a class of objects. Each word is therefore already a generalization. Generalization is a verbal act of thought and reflects reality in quite another way than sensation and perception reflect it. Such a qualitative difference is implied in the proposition that there is a dialectic leap not only between total absence of consciousness (in inanimate matter) and sensation but also between sensation and thought. There is every reason to suppose that the qualitative distinction between sensation and thought is the presence in the latter of a *generalized* reflection of reality, which is also the essence of word meaning; and consequently that meaning is an act of thought in the full sense of the term. But at the same time, meaning is an inalienable part of word as such, and thus it belongs in the realm of language as much as in the realm of thought. A word without meaning is an empty sound, no longer a part of human speech. Since word meaning is both thought and speech, we find in it the unit of verbal thought we are looking for. Clearly, then, the method to follow in our exploration of the nature of verbal thought is semantic analysis — the study of the development, the functioning, and the structure of this unit, which contains thought and speech interrelated.

This method combines the advantages of analysis and synthesis, and it permits adequate study of complex wholes. As an illustration, let us take yet another aspect of our subject, also largely neglected in the past. The primary function of speech is communication, social intercourse. When language was studied through analysis into elements, this function, too, was dissociated from the intellectual function of speech. The two were treated as though they were separate, if parallel, functions, without attention to their structural and developmental inter-relation. Yet word meaning is a unit of both these functions of speech. That understanding between minds is impossible without some mediating expression is an axiom for scientific psychology. In the absence of a system of signs, linguistic or other, only the most primitive and limited type of communica-tion is possible. Communication by means of expressive move-ments, observed mainly among animals, is not so much com-munication as a spread of affect. A frightened goose suddenly aware of danger and rousing the whole flock with its cries does not tell the others what it has seen but rather contaminates them with its fear.

Rational, intentional conveying of experience and thought to others requires a mediating system, the prototype of which is human speech born of the need of intercourse during work. In accordance with the dominant trend, psychology has until recently depicted the matter in an oversimplified way. It was assumed that the means of communication was the sign (the word or sound); that through simultaneous occurrence a sound could become associated with the content of any experience and then serve to convey the same content to other human beings.

Closer study of the development of understanding and com-munication in childhood, however, has led to the conclusion that real communication requires meaning — i.e., generalization — as much as signs. According to Edward Sapir's penetrating description, the world of experience must be greatly simplified and generalized before it can be translated into symbols. Only in this way does communication become possible, for the in-dividual's experience resides only in his own consciousness and is, strictly speaking, not communicable. To become communicable it must be included in a certain category which, by tacit convention, human society regards as a unit.

Thus, true human communication presupposes a generalizing attitude, which is an advanced stage in the development of word meanings. The higher forms of human intercourse are possible only because man's thought reflects conceptualized actuality. That is why certain thoughts cannot be communicated to children even if they are familiar with the necessary words. The adequately generalized concept that alone ensures full understanding may still be lacking. Tolstoy, in his educational writings, says that children often have difficulty in learning a new word not because of its sound but because of the concept to which the word refers. There is a word available nearly always when the concept has matured.

The conception of word meaning as a unit of both generalizing thought and social interchange is of incalculable value for the study of thought and language. It permits true causal-genetic analysis, systematic study of the relations between the growth of the child's thinking ability and his social development. The interrelation of generalization and communication may be considered a secondary focus of our study.

It may be well to mention here some of the problems in the area of language that were not specifically explored in our studies. Foremost among them is the relation of the phonetic aspect of speech to meaning. We believe that the recent important advances in linguistics are largely due to the changes in the method of analysis employed in the study of speech. Traditional linguistics, with its conception of sound as an independent element of speech, used the single sound as the unit of analysis. As a result, it concentrated on the physiology and the acoustics rather than the psychology of speech. Modern linguistics uses the phoneme, the smallest indivisible phonetic unit affecting meaning and thus characteristic of human speech as distinguished from other sounds. Its introduction as the unit of analysis has benefited psychology as well as linguistics. The concrete gains achieved by the application of this method conclusively prove its value. Essentially, it is identical with the method of analysis into units, as distinguished from elements, used in our own investigation.

The fruitfulness of our method may be demonstrated also in other questions concerning relations between functions or between consciousness as a whole and its parts. A brief reference to at least one of these questions will indicate a direction our future studies may take, and point up the import of the present study. We have in mind the relation between intellect and affect. Their separation as subjects of study is a major weakness of traditional psychology since it makes the thought process appear as an autonomous flow of "thoughts thinking themselves," segregated from the fullness of life, from the personal needs and interests, the inclinations and impulses, of the thinker. Such segregated thought must be viewed either as a meaningless epiphenomenon incapable of changing anything in the life or conduct of a person or else as some kind of primeval force exerting an influence on personal life in an inexplicable, mysterious way. The door is closed on the issue of the causation and origin of our thoughts, since deterministic analysis would require clarification of the motive forces that direct thought into this or that channel. By the same token, the old approach precludes any fruitful study of the reverse process, the influence of thought on affect and volition.

Unit analysis points the way to the solution of these vitally important problems. It demonstrates the existence of a dynamic system of meaning in which the affective and the intellectual unite. It shows that every idea contains a transmuted affective attitude toward the bit of reality to which it refers. It further permits us to trace the path from a person's needs and impulses to the specific direction taken by his thoughts, and the reverse path from his thoughts to his behavior and activity. This example should suffice to show that the method used in this study of thought and language is also a promising tool for investigating the relation of verbal thought to consciousness as a whole and to its other essential functions.

2

Piaget's Theory
of Child Language and Thought*

I

PSYCHOLOGY owes a great deal to Jean Piaget. It is not an exaggeration to say that he revolutionized the study of child language and thought. He developed the clinical method of exploring children's ideas which has since been widely used. He was the first to investigate child perception and logic systematically; moreover, he brought to his subject a fresh approach of unusual amplitude and boldness. Instead of listing the deficiencies of child reasoning compared with that of adults, Piaget concentrated on the distinctive characteristics of child thought, on what the child *has* rather than on what the child lacks. Through this positive approach he demonstrated that the difference between child and adult thinking was *qualitative* rather than quantitative.

Like many another great discovery, Piaget's idea is simple to the point of seeming self-evident. It had already been expressed in the words of Rousseau, which Piaget himself quoted, that a child is not a miniature adult and his mind not the mind of an adult on a small scale. Behind this truth, for which Piaget

* This chapter is an abbreviated version of the preface written by Vygotsky for the Russian edition of Piaget's first two books (Gosizdat, Moscow, 1932). Vygotsky's criticism, based on Piaget's early work, is hardly applicable to Piaget's later formulations of his theories — *Editor*

9

provided experimental proof, stands another simple idea — the idea of evolution, which suffuses all of Piaget's studies with a brilliant light.

For all its greatness, however, Piaget's work suffers from the duality common to all the pathfinding contemporary works in psychology. This cleavage is a concomitant of the crisis that psychology is undergoing as it develops into a science in the true sense of the word. The crisis stems from the sharp contradiction between the factual material of science and its methodological and theoretical premises, which have long been a subject of dispute between materialistic and idealistic world conceptions. The struggle is perhaps more acute in psychology than in any other discipline.

As long as we lack a generally accepted system incorporating all the available psychological knowledge, any important factual discovery inevitably leads to the creation of a new theory to fit the newly observed facts. Freud, Levy-Bruhl, Blondel, each created his own system of psychology. The prevailing duality is reflected in the incongruity between these theoretical structures, with their metaphysical, idealistic overtones, and the empiric bases on which they are erected. In modern psychology great discoveries are made daily, only to be shrouded in *ad hoc* theories, prescientific and semimetaphysical.

Piaget tries to escape this fatal duality by sticking to facts. He deliberately avoids generalizing even in his own field and is especially careful not to step over into the related realms of logic, of the theory of cognition, or of the history of philosophy. Pure empiricism seems to him the only safe ground. His book, he writes, is

> first and foremost a collection of facts and documents. The bonds uniting the various chapters are those that a single method can give to diverse findings — by no means those of systematic exposition [29, p. 1].

Indeed, his forte is the unearthing of new facts, their painstaking analysis, their classification — the ability, as Claparède puts it, to *listen* to their message. An avalanche of facts, great and small, opening up new vistas or adding to previous knowledge, tumbles down on child psychology from the pages of Piaget. His clinical method proves a truly invaluable tool for studying the complex structural wholes of child thought in its evolutional transformations. It unifies his diverse investigations and gives us coherent, detailed, real-life pictures of child thinking.

The new facts and the new method led to many problems, some entirely new to scientific psychology, others appearing in a new light. Problems gave birth to theories, in spite of Piaget's determination to avoid them by closely following the experimental facts and disregarding for the time being that the choice itself of experiments is determined by hypotheses. But facts are always examined in the light of some theory and therefore cannot be disentangled from philosophy. This is especially true of facts relative to thinking. To find the key to Piaget's rich store of data we must first explore the philosophy behind his search for facts — and behind their interpretation, which he presents only at the end of his second book [*30*] in a résumé of its contents.

Piaget approaches this task by raising the question of the objective interrelatedness of all the characteristic traits of child thinking he observed. Are these traits fortuitous and independent, or do they form an orderly whole, with a logic of its own, around some central, unifying fact? Piaget believes that they do. In answering the question, he passes from facts to theory, and incidentally shows how much his analysis of facts was influenced by theory, even though in his presentation the theory follows the findings.

According to Piaget, the bond uniting all the specific characteristics of child logic is the egocentrism of the child's thinking. To this core trait he relates all the other traits he found, such as intellectual realism, syncretism, and difficulty in understanding relations. He describes egocentrism as occupying an intermediate position, genetically, structurally, and functionally, between autistic and directed thought.

The idea of the polarity of directed and undirected thought is borrowed from psychoanalytical theory. Piaget says:

Directed thought is conscious, i.e., it pursues aims that are present in the mind of the thinker. It is intelligent, i.e., it is adapted to reality and strives to influence it. It is susceptible of truth and of error . . . and it can be communicated through language. Autistic thought is subconscious, i.e., the goals it pursues and the problems it sets itself are not present in consciousness. It is not adapted to external reality but creates for itself a reality of imagination or dreams. It tends, not to establish truths, but to gratify wishes and remains strictly individual and incommunicable as such by means of language, since it operates primarily in images and must, in order to be communicated, resort to roundabout methods, evoking, by means of symbols and of myths, the feelings that guide it [*29*, pp. 59-60].

Directed thought is social. As it develops, it is increasingly influenced by the laws of experience and of logic proper. Autistic thought, on the contrary, is individualistic and obeys a set of special laws of its own.

Between these two contrasting modes of thought

there are many varieties in regard to their degree of communicability. These intermediate varieties must obey a special logic, intermediate too between the logic of autism and the logic of intelligence. We propose to give the name of *egocentric thought* to the principal of these intermediate forms [*29*, p. 62].

While its main function is still the satisfaction of personal needs, it already includes some mental adaptation, some of the reality orientation typical of the thought of adults. The egocentric thought of the child "stands midway between autism in the strict sense of the word and socialized thought" [*30*, p. 276]. This is Piaget's basic hypothesis.

It is important to note that throughout his work Piaget stresses the traits that egocentric thought has in common with autism rather than the traits that divide them. In the summary at the end of his book, he states emphatically: "Play, when all is said and done, is the supreme law of egocentric thought" [*30*, p. 323]. The same tendency is especially pronounced in his treatment of syncretism, even though he notes that the mechanism of syncretic thinking represents a transition from the logic of dreams to the logic of thought.

Piaget holds that egocentrism stands between extreme autism and the logic of reason chronologically as well as structurally and functionally. His conception of the development of thought is based on the premise taken from psychoanalysis that child thought is originally and naturally autistic and changes to realistic thought only under long and sustained social pressure. This does not, Piaget points out, devaluate the intelligence of the child. "Logical activity isn't all there is to intelligence" [*30*, p. 267]. Imagination is important for finding solutions to problems, but it does not take care of verification and proof, which the search for truth presupposes. The need to verify our thought — that is, the need for logical activity — arises late. This lag is to be expected, says Piaget, since thought begins to serve immediate satisfaction much earlier than to seek for truth; the most spontaneous form of thinking is play, or wishful imaginings that make the desired seem obtainable. Up to the age of seven or eight, play dominates in child thought to such an extent that it is very hard to tell deliberate invention from fantasy that the child believes to be the truth.

To sum up, autism is seen as the original, earliest form of thought; logic appears relatively late; and egocentric thought is the genetic link between them.

This conception, though never presented by Piaget in a coherent, systematic fashion, is the cornerstone of his whole theoretical edifice. True, he states more than once that the assumption of the intermediate nature of child thought is hypothetical, but he also says that this hypothesis is so close to common sense that it seems little more debatable to him than the fact itself of child egocentrism. He traces egocentrism to the nature of the practical activity of the child and to the late development of social attitudes.

> Clearly, from the genetic point of view, one must start from the child's activity in order to understand his thought; and his activity is unquestionably egocentric and egotistic. The social instinct in well-defined form develops late. The first critical period in this respect occurs toward the age of 7 or 8 [*30*, p. 276].

Before this age, Piaget tends to see egocentrism as all-pervading. All the phenomena of child logic in their rich variety he considers directly or indirectly egocentric. Of syncretism, an important expression of egocentrism, he says unequivocally that it permeates the child's entire thinking, both in the verbal and in the perceptual sphere. After seven or eight, when socialized thinking begins to take shape, the egocentric features do not suddenly vanish. They disappear from the child's perceptual operations but remain crystallized in the more abstract area of purely verbal thought.

His conception of the prevalence of egocentrism in childhood leads Piaget to conclude that egocentrism of thought is so intimately related to the child's psychic nature that it is impervious to experience. The influences to which adults subject the child

> are not imprinted on him as on a photographic plate: They are "assimilated," that is to say, deformed by the living being subjected to them and become implanted in his own substance. It is this psychological substance of the child or, in other words, the structure and the functioning peculiar to child thought that we have endeavored to describe and, in a measure, to explain [*30*, p. 338].

This passage epitomizes the nature of Piaget's basic assumptions and brings us to the general problem of social and biological uniformities in psychic development, to which we shall return in Section III. First, let us examine the soundness of Piaget's conception of child egocentrism in the light of the facts on which it is based.

II

Since Piaget's conception of child egocentrism is of primary significance in his theory, we must inquire what facts led him not only to accept it as a hypothesis but to put such great faith in it. We shall then test these facts by comparing them with the results of our own experiments. [*46, 47*].

The factual basis of Piaget's belief is provided by his investigation of the child's use of language. His systematic observations led him to conclude that all conversations of children fall into two groups, the egocentric and the socialized. The dif-

ference between them lies mainly in their functions. In egocentric speech, the child talks only about himself, takes no interest in his interlocutor, does not try to communicate, expects
no answers, and often does not even care whether anyone listens
to him. It is similar to a monologue in a play: The child is
thinking aloud, keeping up a running accompaniment, as it
were, to whatever he may be doing. In socialized speech, he
does attempt an exchange with others — he begs, commands,
threatens, conveys information, asks questions.

Piaget's experiments showed that by far the greater part
of the preschool child's talk is egocentric. He found that from
44 to 47 per cent of the total recorded talk of children in their
seventh year was egocentric in nature. This figure, he says,
must be considerably increased in the case of younger children.
Further investigations with six- and seven-year-olds proved that
even socialized speech at that age is not entirely free of egocentric thinking. Furthermore, besides his expressed thoughts the
child has a great many unexpressed thoughts. Some of these,
according to Piaget, remain unexpressed precisely because they
are egocentric, i.e., incommunicable. To convey them to others
the child would have to be able to adopt their point of view.
"One might say that an adult thinks socially even when he is
alone, and a child under seven thinks and speaks egocentrically
even in the society of others" [29, p. 56]. Thus the coefficient of
egocentric thought must be much higher than the coefficient
of egocentric speech. But it is the data on speech, which can
be measured, that furnish the documentary proof on which
Piaget bases his conception of child egocentrism. His explanations of egocentric speech and of child egocentrism in general
are identical.

> In the first place, there is no sustained social life among children
> of less than 7 or 8; in the second place, the real social language
> of the child, that is, the language used in the basic activity of
> children — play — is a language of gestures, movements, and mimi-
> cry as much as of words [29, p. 56].

When, at the age of seven or eight, the desire to work with
others manifests itself, egocentric talk subsides.

In his description of egocentric speech and its developmental fate, Piaget emphasizes that it does not fulfill any realistically useful function in the child's behavior and that it simply atrophies as the child approaches school age. Our own experiments suggest a different conception. We believe that egocentric speech early assumes a very definite and important role in the activity of the child.

In order to determine what causes egocentric talk, what circumstances provoke it, we organized the children's activities in much the same way Piaget did, but we added a series of frustrations and difficulties. For instance, when a child was getting ready to draw, he would suddenly find that there was no paper, or no pencil of the color he needed. In other words, by obstructing his free activity we made him face problems.*

We found that in these difficult situations the coefficient of egocentric speech almost doubled, in comparison with Piaget's normal figure for the same age and also in comparison with our figure for children not facing these problems. The child would try to grasp and to remedy the situation in talking to himself: "Where's the pencil? I need a blue pencil. Never mind, I'll draw with the red one and wet it with water; it will become dark and look like blue."

In the same activities without impediments, our coefficient of egocentric talk was even slightly lower than Piaget's. It is legitimate to assume, then, that a disruption in the smooth flow of activity is an important stimulus for egocentric speech. This discovery fits in with two premises to which Piaget himself refers several times in his book. One of them is the so-called law of awareness, which states that an impediment or disturbance in an automatic activity makes the actor aware of that activity. The other premise is that speech is an expression of that process of becoming aware.

Our findings indicate that egocentric speech does not long remain a mere accompaniment to the child's activity. Besides being a means of expression and of release of tension, it soon becomes an instrument of thought in the proper sense — in seeking and planning the solution of a problem. An accident that occurred during one of our experiments provides a good illus-

* See Chapter 7 for other aspects of these experiments.

tration of one way in which egocentric speech may alter the course of an activity: A child of five and a half was drawing a streetcar when the point of his pencil broke. He tried, nevertheless, to finish the circle of a wheel, pressing down on the pencil very hard, but nothing showed on the paper except a deep colorless line. The child muttered to himself, "It's broken," put aside the pencil, took watercolors instead, and began drawing a *broken* streetcar after an accident, continuing to talk to himself from time to time about the change in his picture. The child's accidentally provoked egocentric utterance so manifestly affected his activity that it is impossible to mistake it for a mere by-product, an accompaniment not interfering with the melody. Our experiments showed highly complex changes in the interrelation of activity and egocentric talk. We observed how egocentric speech at first marked the end result or a turning point in an activity, then was gradually shifted toward the middle and finally to the beginning of the activity, taking on a directing, planning function and raising the child's acts to the level of purposeful behavior. What happens here is similar to the well-known developmental sequence in the naming of drawings. A small child draws first, then decides what it is that he has drawn; at a slightly older age, he names his drawing when it is half done; and finally he decides beforehand what he will draw.

The revised conception of the function of egocentric speech must also influence our conception of its later fate and must be brought to bear on the issue of its disappearance at school age. Experiments can yield indirect evidence but no conclusive answer about the causes of this disappearance. Nevertheless, the data obtained strongly suggest the hypothesis that egocentric speech is a transitional stage in the evolution from vocal to inner speech. The older children in our experiments behaved differently from the younger ones when faced with obstacles. Often the child examined the situation in silence, then found a solution. When asked what he was thinking about, he gave answers that were quite close to the thinking-aloud of the preschooler. This would indicate that the same mental operations that the preschooler carries out through egocentric speech are already relegated to soundless inner speech in the schoolchild.

There is, of course, nothing to this effect in Piaget, who believes that egocentric speech simply dies off. The development of inner speech in the child receives little specific elucidation in his studies. But since inner speech and voiced egocentric speech fulfill the same function, the implication would be that if, as Piaget maintains, egocentric speech precedes socialized speech then inner speech also must precede socialized speech — an assumption untenable from the genetic point of view.

The inner speech of the adult represents his "thinking for himself" rather than social adaptation; i.e., it has the same function that egocentric speech has in the child. It also has the same structural characteristics: Out of context, it would be incomprehensible to others because it omits to "mention" what is obvious to the "speaker." These similarities lead us to assume that when egocentric speech disappears from view it does not simply atrophy but "goes underground," i.e., turns into inner speech. Our observation that at the age when this change is taking place children facing difficult situations resort now to egocentric speech, now to silent reflection, indicates that the two can be functionally equivalent. It is our hypothesis that the processes of inner speech develop and become stabilized approximately at the beginning of school age and that this causes the quick drop in egocentric speech observed at that stage.

Limited in scope as our findings are, we believe that they help one to see in a new and broader perspective the general direction of the development of speech and thought. In Piaget's view, the two functions follow a common path, from autistic to socialized speech, from subjective fantasy to the logic of relationships. In the course of this change, the influence of adults is deformed by the psychic processes of the child, but it wins out in the end. The development of thought is, to Piaget, a story of the gradual socialization of deeply intimate, personal, autistic mental states. Even social speech is represented as following, not preceding, egocentric speech.

The hypothesis we propose reverses this course. Let us look

at the direction of thought development during one short interval, from the appearance of egocentric speech to its disappearance, in the framework of language development as a whole.

We consider that the total development runs as follows: The primary function of speech, in both children and adults, is communication, social contact. The earliest speech of the child is therefore essentially social. At first it is global and multifunctional; later its functions become differentiated. At a certain age the social speech of the child is quite sharply divided into egocentric and communicative speech. (We prefer to use the term *communicative* for the form of speech that Piaget calls *socialized* as though it had been something else before becoming social. From our point of view, the two forms, communicative and egocentric, are both social, though their functions differ.) Egocentric speech emerges when the child transfers social, collaborative forms of behavior to the sphere of inner-personal psychic functions. The child's tendency to transfer to his inner processes the behavior patterns that formerly were social is well known to Piaget. He describes in another context how arguments between children give rise to the beginnings of logical reflection. Something similar happens, we believe, when the child starts conversing with himself as he has been doing with others. When circumstances force him to stop and think, he is likely to think aloud. Egocentric speech, splintered off from general social speech, in time leads to inner speech, which serves both autistic and logical thinking.

Egocentric speech as a separate linguistic form is the highly important genetic link in the transition from vocal to inner speech, an intermediate stage between the differentiation of the functions of vocal speech and the final transformation of one part of vocal speech into inner speech. It is this transitional role of egocentric speech that lends it such great theoretical interest. The whole conception of speech development differs profoundly in accordance with the interpretation given to the role of egocentric speech. Thus our schema of development — first social, then egocentric, then inner speech — contrasts both with the traditional behaviorist schema — vocal speech, whisper, inner speech — and with Piaget's sequence — from nonverbal autistic thought through egocentric thought and speech to socialized speech and logical thinking. In our conception, the true direction of the development of thinking is not from the individual to the socialized, but from the social to the individual.

III

It is not possible within the limits of the present study to evaluate all aspects of Piaget's theory of intellectual development; our interest focuses on his conception of the role of egocentrism in the developmental relationship of language and thought. We shall, however, point out briefly those of his basic theoretical and methodological assumptions which we consider erroneous, as well as the facts he fails to take into account in his characterization of child thinking.

Modern psychology in general, and child psychology in particular, reveal a tendency to combine psychological and philosophical issues. A subject of the German psychologist Ach aptly summarized this trend when he remarked at the end of a session, "But that is experimental philosophy!" And indeed many issues in the complex field of child thinking border on the theory of cognition, on theoretical logic, and on other branches of philosophy. Time and again Piaget inadvertently touches upon one or another of these but with remarkable consistency checks himself and breaks off. Yet in spite of his express intention to avoid theorizing, he does not succeed in keeping his work within the bounds of pure factual science. Deliberate avoidance of philosophy is itself a philosophy, and one that may involve its proponents in many inconsistencies. An example of this is Piaget's view of the place of causal explanation in science.

Piaget attempts to refrain from considering causes in presenting his findings. In doing so, he comes dangerously close to what he calls, in the child, "precausality," though he himself may view his abstention as a sophisticated "supracausal" stage, in which the concept of causality has been outgrown. He proposes to replace the explanation of phenomena in terms of cause and effect by a genetic analysis in terms of temporal sequence and by the application of a mathematically conceived formula of the functional interdependence of phenomena. In the case of two interdependent phenomena, A and B, A may be viewed as a function of B, or B as a function of A. The investigator reserves the right to organize his description of the data in the way that best suits his purpose at the time, although he will usually give preferential position to the earlier developmental phenomena as being more explanatory in the genetic sense.

This substitution of the functional for the causal interpretation deprives the concept of development of any real content. Even though Piaget, in discussing the biological and the social factors, acknowledges that the student of mental development is duty-bound to explain the relation between them and to neglect neither, his solution is as follows:

> But, to begin, it is necessary to choose one of the idioms to the disadvantage of the other. We have chosen the sociological idiom, but we emphasize that there is nothing exclusive about this — we reserve the right to return to the biological explanation of child thought and to translate into its terms the description we are attempting here [*30*, p. 266].

This indeed makes Piaget's whole approach a matter of purely arbitrary choice.

The basic framework of Piaget's theory rests on the assumption of a genetic sequence of two opposite forms of mentation which are described by the psychoanalytic theory as serving the pleasure principle and the reality principle. From our point of view, the drive for the satisfaction of needs and the drive for adaptation to reality cannot be considered separate from and opposed to each other. A need can be truly satisfied only through a certain adaptation to reality. Moreover, there is no such thing as adaptation for the sake of adaptation; it is always directed by needs. That is a truism inexplicably overlooked by Piaget.

Piaget shares with Freud not only the untenable conception of a pleasure principle preceding a reality principle but also the metaphysical approach which elevates the desire for pleasure from its true status of a biologically important ancillary factor to that of an independent vital force, the prime mover of psychic development. Once he has separated need and pleasure from adaptation to reality, logic forces Piaget to present realistic thought as standing apart from concrete needs, interests, and wishes, as "pure thought" whose function is the search for truth exclusively for its own sake.

Autistic thought — the original opposite of realistic thought in Piaget's scheme — is, in our opinion, a late development, a result of realistic thought and of its corollary, thinking in concepts, which leads to a degree of autonomy from reality and thus permits satisfaction in fantasy of the needs frustrated in life. This conception of autism is consistent with Bleuler's [3]. Autism is one of the effects of the differentiation and polarization of the various functions of thought.

Our experiments brought to the fore another important point overlooked so far: the role of the child's activity in the evolution of his thought processes. We have seen that egocentric speech is not suspended in a void but is directly related to the child's practical dealings with the real world. We have seen that it enters as a constituent part into the process of rational activity, taking on intelligence, as it were, from the child's incipiently purposeful actions; and that it increasingly serves problem-solving and planning as the child's activities grow more complex. This process is set in motion by the child's actions; the objects he deals with mean reality and shape his thought processes.

In the light of these facts, Piaget's conclusions call for clarification concerning two important points. First, the peculiarities of child thought discussed by Piaget, such as syncretism, do not extend over quite so large an area as Piaget believes. We are inclined to think (and our experiments bear us out) that the child thinks syncretically in matters of which he has no knowledge or experience but does not resort to syncretism in relation to familiar things or things within easy reach of practical checking — and the number of these things depends on the method of education. Also, within syncretism itself we must expect to find some precursors of the future causal con-

ceptions which Piaget himself mentions in passing. The syncretic schemata themselves, despite their fluctuations, lead the
child gradually toward adaptation; their usefulness must not
be underrated. Sooner or later, through strict selection, reduction, and mutual adaptation, they will be sharpened into excellent tools of investigation in areas where hypotheses are
of use.

The second point which calls for reappraisal and limitation
is the applicability of Piaget's findings to children in general.
His experiments led him to believe that the child was impervious to experience. Piaget draws an analogy which we find
illuminating: Primitive man, he says, learns from experience
only in a few special, limited cases of practical activity — and
he cites as examples of these rare cases agriculture, hunting,
and manufacturing things.

> But this ephemeral, partial contact with reality does not in the
> least affect the general trend of his thinking. The same is all the
> more true of children [*30*, pp. 268-269].

We would not call agriculture and hunting negligible contacts
with reality in the case of primitive man; they are practically
his whole existence. Piaget's view may hold true for the particular group of children he studied, but it is not of universal
significance. He himself tells us the cause of the special quality
of thinking he observed in his children:

> The child never really and truly comes in contact with things,
> because he does not work. He plays with things, or takes them for
> granted [*30*, p. 269].

The developmental uniformities established by Piaget apply
to the given milieu, under the conditions of Piaget's study.
They are not laws of nature but are historically and socially
determined. Piaget has already been criticized by Stern for his
failure sufficiently to take into account the importance of the
social situation and milieu. Whether the child's talk is more
egocentric or more social depends not only on his age but also
on the surrounding conditions. Piaget observed children at play
together in a particular kindergarten, and his coefficients are

valid only for this special child milieu. When the children's activity consists entirely of play, it is accompanied by extensive soliloquizing. Stern points out that in a German kindergarten, in which there was more group activity, the coefficient of egocentrism was somewhat lower, and that in the home children's speech tends to be predominantly social at a very early age. If that is true of German children, the difference between Soviet children and Piaget's children in the Geneva kindergarten must be even greater. Piaget admits, in his foreword to the Russian edition of his book, that it is necessary to compare the behavior of children of different social backgrounds to be able to distinguish the social from the individual in their thinking. For this reason he welcomes collaboration with Soviet psychologists. We, too, are convinced that the study of thought development in children from a different social environment, and especially of children who, unlike Piaget's children, work, must lead to results that will permit the formulation of laws having a much wider sphere of application.

3

Stern's Theory of Language Development

THE PART of William Stern's system that is best known and has actually gained ground over the years is his intellectualistic conception of speech development in the child. Yet it is precisely this conception that plainly reveals the limitations and inconsistencies of Stern's philosophical and psychological personalism, its idealistic foundations and scientific invalidity.

Stern himself describes his point of view as "personalistic-genetic." We shall discuss the personalistic principle later on. Let us see first how Stern deals with the genetic aspect, and let us state from the outset that his theory, like all intellectualistic theories, is by its very nature antidevelopmental.

Stern distinguishes three roots of speech: the expressive tendency, the social, and the "intentional." While the first two underlie also the rudiments of speech observed in animals, the third is specifically human. Stern defines *intentionality* in this sense as a directedness toward a certain content, or meaning. "At a certain stage of his psychic development," he says, "man acquires the ability to mean something when uttering sounds, to refer to something objective" [*38*, p. 126]. In substance, such intentional acts are already acts of thought; their appearance denotes intellectualization and objectification of speech.

In agreement with a number of writers who represent the new psychology of thought, though to a lesser degree than some of them, Stern stresses the importance of the logical factor in the development of language.

We have no quarrel with the statement that advanced human speech possesses objective meaning and therefore presupposes a certain level in the development of thinking, and we agree that it is necessary to take account of the close relationship that exists between language and logical thinking. The trouble is that Stern regards intentionality, a trait of advanced speech which properly calls for a genetic explanation (i.e., how it came into being in the evolutionary process), as one of the *roots* of speech development, a driving force, an innate tendency, almost an urge, at any rate something primordial, on a par genetically with the expressive and the communicative tendencies — which indeed are found at the very beginnings of speech. In viewing intentionality in this way (*"die 'intentionale' Triebfeder des Sprachdranges"*), he substitutes an intellectualistic explanation for the genetic one.

This method of "explaining" a thing by the very thing that needs explaining is the basic flaw of all intellectualistic theories and of Stern's in particular — hence its general hollowness and its antigenetic quality (traits belonging to advanced speech are relegated to its beginnings). Stern answers the question of why and how speech acquires meaning by saying: from the intentional tendency, i.e., the tendency toward meaning. We are reminded of Molière's physician who explained the soporific effect of opium by its soporific properties.

From Stern's famous description of the great discovery made by the child of one and a half or two, we can see to what exaggerations overemphasis on the logical aspects can lead. At that age the child first realizes that each object has its permanent symbol, a sound pattern that identifies it — i.e., that each thing has *a name*. Stern believes that a child in the second year of his life can become aware of symbols and of the need for them, and he considers this discovery already a thought process in the proper sense:

> The understanding of the relation between sign and meaning that dawns on the child at this point is something different in principle from the simple use of sound images, object images,

and their associations. And the requirement that *each* object of whatever kind have its name may be considered a true generalization made by the child — possibly his first [*40*, pp. 109-110].

Are there any factual and theoretical grounds for assuming that a child of one and a half or two has an awareness of the symbolic function of language and a consciousness of a general rule, a general concept? All the studies made of this problem in the last twenty years suggest a negative answer to this question.

Everything we know of the mentality of the child of one and a half or two clashes with the idea that he might be capable of such complex intellectual operations. Both observation and experimental studies indicate that he grasps only much later the relationship between sign and meaning, or the functional use of signs; this is quite beyond a child of two. Furthermore, systematic experimental investigations have shown that the grasping of the relation between sign and meaning, and the transition to operating with signs, never result from an instantaneous discovery or invention by the child. Stern believes that the child discovers the meaning of language once and for all. Actually, this is an extremely complex process which has its "natural history" (i.e., its early beginnings and transitional forms on the more primitive developmental levels) and also its "cultural history" (again with its own series of phases, its own quantitative, qualitative, and functional growth, its own dynamics and laws).

Stern virtually ignores the intricate ways leading to the ripening of the sign function; his conception of linguistic development is immensely simplified. The child suddenly discovers that speech has meaning: Such an explanation of how speech becomes meaningful truly deserves to be grouped with the theory of the deliberate invention of language, the rationalistic theory of the social contract, and other famous intellectualistic theories. All of them disregard the genetic realities and do not really explain anything.

Factually, too, Stern's theory fails to stand up. Wallon, Koffka, Piaget, Delacroix, and many others in their studies of normal children, and K. Buehler in his study of deaf-mute children, have found (1) that the discovery by the child of the tie between word and object does *not* immediately lead to a clear awareness of the symbolic relationship of sign and referent, characteristic of well-developed thought; that the word for a long time appears to the child as an attribute or a property of the object rather than as a mere sign; that the child grasps the external structure object-word before he can grasp the internal relation sign-referent; and (2) that the discovery made by the child is not in reality a sudden one, the exact instant of which can be defined. A series of long and complicated "molecular" changes leads up to that critical moment in speech development.

That Stern's basic observation was correct, that there is indeed a moment of discovery which to gross observation appears unprepared, has been established beyond doubt during the twenty years since his study was first published. The decisive turning point in the child's linguistic, cultural, and intellectual development discovered by Stern does exist — though he was wrong to interpret it intellectualistically. Stern points out two objective symptoms of the occurrence of the critical change: the appearance of inquiries about names of objects and the resulting sharp, saccadic increases in the child's vocabulary, both of major importance for the development of speech.

The active search for words on the part of the child, which has no analogy in the development of "speech" in animals, indicates a new phase in his linguistic progress. It is at this time that the "grandiose signal system of speech" (to quote Pavlov) emerges for the child from the mass of all other signals and assumes a specific function in behavior. To have established this fact on a firm basis of objective symptoms is one of Stern's great achievements. The gap in his explanation of it is all the more striking.

In contrast with the two other roots of language, the expressive and the communicative, whose development has been traced from the lowest social animals to anthropoids and to man, the "intentional tendency" appears out of nowhere; it has no history and no derivation. According to Stern, it is basic, primordial; it springs up spontaneously "once and for all." This is the propensity enabling the child to discover the function of speech by way of a purely logical operation.

To be sure, Stern does not say all this in so many words. He engaged in polemics not only with the proponents of anti-intellectualistic theories who trace the beginnings of speech in children to affective-conative processes exclusively, but also with those psychologists who overrate the child's capacity for logical thinking. Stern does not repeat that mistake, but he makes a graver one in assigning to intellect an almost metaphysical position of primacy as the origin, the unanalyzable first cause of meaningful speech.

Paradoxically, intellectualism of this kind proves especially inadequate in the study of intellectual processes, which at first glance would seem to be its legitimate sphere of application. One might expect, for instance, that much light would be thrown on the relation between speech and thought when the meaningfulness of language is regarded as a result of an intellectual operation. Actually, such an approach, stipulating as it does an *already formed* intellect, blocks an investigation of the involved dialectical interactions of thought and speech. Stern's treatment of this cardinal aspect of the problem of language is full of inconsistencies and is the weakest part of his book [*38*].

Such important topics as inner speech, its emergence, and its connection with thought are barely touched upon by Stern. He reviews the results of Piaget's investigation of egocentric speech merely in his discussion of children's conversations, ignoring the functions, the structure, and the developmental significance of that form of speech. Altogether, Stern fails to relate the complex functional and structural changes in thinking to the development of speech.

Even when Stern gives a correct characterization of a developmental phenomenon, his theoretical framework prevents him from drawing the obvious conclusions from his own observations. Nowhere is this fact more apparent than in his failure to see the implications of his own "translation" of the child's very first words into the language of adults. The interpretation given to the first words of the child is the touchstone of every theory of child speech; it is the focal point at which all the major trends in modern speech theories meet and cross. One might say without exaggeration that the whole structure of a theory is determined by the translation of the first words of the child.

Stern believes that they should be interpreted neither from the purely intellectualistic nor from the purely affective-conative point of view. He acknowledges Meumann's great merit in opposing the intellectualistic theory that the child's first words actually designate objects as such [28]. He does not, however, share Meumann's assumption that the first words are merely expressions of the emotions and wishes of the child. Through his analysis of situations in which they appear, he proves quite conclusively that these words contain also a certain direction toward an object and that this "objective reference" or pointing function often "predominates over the moderately emotional tone" [38, p. 183].

This is how Stern translates first words:

> The childish *mama*, translated into advanced speech, does not mean the word "mother" but rather a sentence such as "Mama, come here," or "Mama, give me," or "Mama, put me in the chair," or "Mama, help me" [38, p. 180].

When we observe the child in action, however, it becomes obvious that it is not only the word *mama* which means, say, "Mama, put me in the chair," but *the child's whole behavior at that moment* (his reaching out toward the chair, trying to hold on to it, etc.). Here the "affective-conative" directedness toward an object (to use Meumann's terms) is as yet inseparable from the "intentional tendency" of speech: The two are still a homogeneous whole, and the only correct translation of *mama*, or of any other early words, is the pointing gesture. The word, at first, is a conventional substitute for the gesture; it appears long before the child's crucial "discovery of language" and before he is capable of logical operations. Stern himself admits the mediatory role of gestures, especially pointing, in establishing the meaning of first words. The inescapable conclusion would be that pointing is, in fact, a precursor of the "intentional tendency." Yet Stern declines to trace the genetic history of that tendency. To him, it does not evolve from the affective object-directedness of the pointing act (gesture or first words) — it appears out of nowhere, and it accounts for the emergence of meaning.

The same antigenetic approach also characterizes Stern's treatment of all the other major issues discussed in his pithy book, such as the development of concepts and the main stages in the development of speech and thought. Nor can it be otherwise: This approach is a direct consequence of the philosophical premises of personalism, the system developed by Stern.

Stern tries to rise above the extremes of both empiricism and nativism. He opposes his own view of the development of speech, on the one hand, to Wundt's, who sees child speech as a product of environment, while the child's own participation is essentially passive, and, on the other hand, to the view of those psychologists to whom primary speech (onomatopoeia and so-called nursery talk) is the invention of countless generations of children. Stern takes care not to disregard the part that imitation plays in speech development, or the role of the child's spontaneous activity, by applying to these issues his concept of "convergence": The child's conquest of speech occurs through a constant interaction of inner dispositions prompting the child to speech and external conditions — i.e., the speech of people around him — which provide both stimulation and material for the realization of these dispositions.

Convergence, to Stern, is a general principle to be applied to the explanation of all human behavior. Truly this is one more instance when we may say, with Goethe, "The words of science hide its substance." The sonorous word *convergence*, denoting here a perfectly unassailable methodological principle (i.e., that development should be studied as a process determined by the interaction of organism and environment), in fact releases the author from the task of analyzing the social, environmental factors in speech development. Stern does say quite emphatically, it is true, that social environment is the main factor in speech development, but in reality he limits its role to merely accelerating or slowing down the development, which obeys its own immanent laws. As we have tried to show by using the example of his explanation of how meaning emerges in speech, Stern greatly overrated the role of the internal organismic factors.

This bias is a direct outcome of the personalistic frame of reference. The "person" to Stern is a psychophysically neutral entity that "in spite of the multiplicity of its part-functions manifests a unitary, goal-directed activity" [39, p. 16]. This idealistic, "monadic" conception of the individual person naturally leads to a theory which sees language as rooted in personal teleology — hence the intellectualism and the antigenetic bias of Stern's approach to problems of linguistic development. Applied to the eminently social mechanism of speech behavior, Stern's personalism, ignoring as it does the social side of personality, leads to patent absurdities. His metaphysical conception of personality, deriving all developmental processes from personal teleology, turns the real genetic relations between personality and language upside down: Instead of a developmental history of the personality itself, in which language plays a far from minor role, we have the metaphysical theory that personality generates language out of the goal-directedness of its own essential nature.

4

The Genetic Roots of Thought and Speech

I

THE MOST important fact uncovered through the genetic study of thought and speech is that their relationship undergoes many changes. Progress in thought and progress in speech are not parallel. Their two growth curves cross and recross. They may straighten out and run side by side, even merge for a time, but they always diverge again. This applies to both phylogeny and ontogeny.

In animals, speech and thought spring from different roots and develop along different lines. This fact is confirmed by Koehler's, Yerkes's, and other recent studies of apes. Koehler's experiments proved that the appearance in animals of an embryonic intellect — i.e., of thinking in the proper sense — is in no way related to speech. The "inventions" of apes in making and using tools, or in finding detours for the solution of problems, though undoubtedly rudimentary thinking, belong in a prelinguistic phase of thought development.

In Koehler's opinion, his investigations prove that the chimpanzee shows the beginnings of an intellectual behavior of the same kind and type as man's. It is the lack of speech, "that infinitely valuable technical aid," and the paucity of images, "that most important intellectual material," which explain the tremendous difference between anthropoids and the most primitive man and make "even the slightest beginnings of cultural

33

development impossible for the chimpanzee" [*18*, pp. 191-192].

There is considerable disagreement among psychologists of different schools about the theoretical interpretation of Koehler's findings. The mass of critical literature that his studies have called forth represents a variety of viewpoints. It is all the more significant that no one disputes Koehler's facts or the deduction which particularly interests us: the independence of the chimpanzee's actions from speech. This is freely admitted even by the psychologists (for example, Thorndike or Borovskij) who do not see anything in the chimpanzee's actions beyond the mechanics of instinct and of "trial-and-error" learning, "nothing at all except the already known process of habit formation" [*4*, p. 179], and by the introspectionists, who shy away from lowering intellect to the level of even the most advanced behavior of apes. Buehler says quite rightly that the actions of the chimpanzees are entirely unconnected with speech; and that in man the thinking involved in the use of tools (*Werkzeugdenken*) also is much less connected with speech and with concepts than are other forms of thought.

The issue would be quite simple if apes had no rudiments of language, nothing at all resembling speech. We do, however, find in the chimpanzee a relatively well-developed "language," in some respects — most of all phonetically — not unlike human speech. The remarkable thing about his language is that it functions apart from his intellect. Koehler, who studied chimpanzees for many years at the Canary Island Anthropoid Station, tells us that their phonetic expressions denote only desires and subjective states; they are expressions of affects, never a sign of anything "objective" [*19*, p. 27]. But chimpanzee and human phonetics have so many elements in common that we may confidently suppose that the absence of humanlike speech is not due to any peripheral causes.

The chimpanzee is an extremely gregarious animal and responds strongly to the presence of others of his kind. Koehler describes highly diversified forms of "linguistic communication" among chimpanzees. First in line is their vast repertory of affective expressions: facial play, gestures, vocalization; next come the movements expressing social emotions: gestures of greeting, etc. The apes are capable both of "understanding" one another's gestures and of "expressing," through gestures, desires involving other animals. Usually a chimpanzee will *begin* a movement or an action he wants another animal to perform or to share — e.g., will push him and execute the initial movements of walking when "inviting" the other to follow him, or grab at the air when he wants the other to give him a banana. All these are gestures *directly* related to the action itself. Koehler mentions that the experimenter comes to use essentially similar elementary ways of communication to convey to the apes what is expected of them.

By and large, these observations confirm Wundt's opinion that pointing gestures, the first stage in the development of human speech, do not yet appear in animals but that some gestures of apes are a transitional form between grasping and pointing [56, p. 219]. We consider this transitional gesture a most important step from unadulterated affective expression toward objective language.

There is no evidence, however, that animals reach the stage of objective representation in any of their activities. Koehler's chimpanzees played with colored clay, "painting" first with lips and tongue, later with real paintbrushes; but these animals — who normally transfer to play the use of tools and other behavior learned "in earnest" (i.e., in experiments) and, conversely, play behavior to "real life" — never exhibited the slightest intent of representing anything in their drawings or the slightest sign of attributing any objective meaning to their products. Buehler says:

> Certain facts warn us against overestimating the chimpanzee's actions. We know that no traveler has ever mistaken a gorilla or a chimpanzee for a man, and that no one has ever observed among them any of the traditional tools or methods that with humans vary from tribe to tribe but indicate the transmission from generation to generation of discoveries once made; no scratchings on sandstone or clay that could be taken for designs representing anything or even for ornaments scratched in play; no representational language, i.e., no sounds equivalent to names. All this together must have some intrinsic causes [7, p. 20].

Yerkes seems to be the only one among modern observers of apes to explain their lack of speech otherwise than by "intrinsic causes." His research on the intellect of orangutans yielded data very similar to Koehler's; but he goes further in his conclusions: He admits "higher ideation" in orangs — on the level, it is true, of a three-year-old child at most [57, p. 132].

Yerkes deduces ideation merely from superficial similarities between anthropoid and human behavior; he has no objective proof that orangs solve problems with the help of ideation, i.e., of "images," or trace stimuli. In the study of the higher animals, analogy may be used to good purpose within the boundaries of objectivity, but basing an assumption on analogy is hardly a scientific procedure.

Koehler, on the other hand, went beyond the mere use of analogy in exploring the nature of the chimpanzee's intellectual processes. He showed by precise experimental analysis that the success of the animals' actions depended on whether they could see all the elements of a situation simultaneously — this was a decisive factor in their behavior. If, especially during the earlier experiments, the stick they used to reach some fruit lying beyond the bars was moved slightly, so that the tool (stick) and the goal (fruit) were not visible to them at one glance, the solution of the problem became very difficult, often impossible. The apes had learned to make a longer tool by inserting one stick into an opening in another. If the two sticks accidentally crossed in their hands, forming an X, they became unable to perform the familiar, much-practiced operation of lengthening the tool. Dozens of similar examples from Koehler's experiments could be cited.

Koehler considers the actual visual presence of a sufficiently simple situation an indispensable condition in any investigation of the intellect of chimpanzees, a condition without which their intellect cannot be made to function at all; he concludes that the inherent limitations of imagery (or "ideation") are a basic feature of the chimpanzee's intellectual behavior. If we accept Koehler's thesis, then Yerkes's assumption appears more than doubtful.

In connection with his recent experimental and observational studies of the intellect and language of chimpanzees, Yerkes presents new material on their linguistic development and a new, ingenious theory to account for their lack of real speech. "Vocal reactions," he says, "are very frequent and varied in young chimpanzees, but speech in the human sense is absent" [*58*, p. 53]. Their vocal apparatus is as well developed and functions as well as man's. What is missing is the tendency to imitate sounds. Their mimicry is almost entirely dependent on optical stimuli; they copy actions but not sounds. They are incapable of doing what the parrot does so successfully.

> If the imitative tendency of the parrot were combined with the caliber of intellect of the chimpanzee, the latter undoubtedly would possess speech, since he has a voice mechanism comparable to man's as well as an intellect of the type and level to enable him to use sounds for purposes of real speech [*58*, p. 53].

In his experiments, Yerkes applied four methods of teaching chimpanzees to speak. None of them succeeded. Such failures, of course, never solve a problem in principle. In this case, we still do not know whether or not it is possible to teach chimpanzees to speak. Not uncommonly the fault lies with the experimenter. Koehler says that if earlier studies of chimpanzee intellect failed to show that he had any, this was not because the chimpanzee really has none but because of inadequate methods, ignorance of the limits of difficulty within which the chimpanzee intellect can manifest itself, ignorance of its dependence on a comprehensive visual situation. "Investigations of intellectual capacity," quipped Koehler, "necessarily test the experimenter as well as the subject" [*18*, p. 191].

Without settling the issue in principle, Yerkes's experiments showed once more that anthropoids do not have anything like human speech, even in embryo. Correlating this with what we know from other sources, we may assume that apes are probably incapable of real speech.

What are the causes of their inability to speak, since they have the necessary voice apparatus and phonetic range? Yerkes sees the cause in the absence or weakness of vocal imitativeness. This may very well have been the immediate cause of the nega-

tive results of his experiments, but he is probably wrong in seeing it as the fundamental cause of the lack of speech in apes.
The latter thesis, though Yerkes presents it as established, is
belied by everything we know of the chimpanzee's intellect.

Yerkes had at his disposal an excellent means of checking
his thesis, which for some reason he did not use and which we
should be only too happy to apply if we had the material possibility. We should exclude the auditory factor in training the
animals in a linguistic skill. Language does not of necessity depend on sound. There are, for instance, the sign language of
deaf-mutes and lip reading, which is also interpretation of
movement. In the languages of primitive peoples, gestures are
used along with sound, and play a substantial role. In principle,
language does not depend on the nature of its material. If it is
true that the chimpanzee has the intellect for acquiring something analogous to human language, and the whole trouble lies
in his lacking vocal imitativeness, then he should be able, in experiments, to master some conventional gestures whose psychological function would be exactly the same as that of conventional sounds. As Yerkes himself conjectures, the chimpanzees might be trained, for instance, to use manual gestures
rather than sounds. The medium is beside the point; what matters is the *functional use of signs,* any signs that could play a role
corresponding to that of speech in humans.

This method has not been tested, and we cannot be sure
what its results might have been; but everything we know of
chimpanzee behavior, including Yerkes's data, dispels the hope
that they could learn functional speech. Not a hint of their using signs has ever been heard of. The only thing we know with
objective certainty is not that they have "ideation" but that
under certain conditions they are able to make very simple tools
and resort to "detours," and that these conditions include a
completely visible, utterly clear situation. In all problems not
involving immediately perceived visual structures but centering
on some other kind of structure — mechanical, for instance —
the chimpanzees switched from an insightful type of behavior
to the trial-end-error method pure and simple.

Are the conditions required for the apes' effective intellectual functioning also the conditions required for discovering speech or discovering the functional use of signs? Definitely not. Discovery of speech cannot, in any situation, depend on an optical setup. It demands an intellectual operation of a different kind. There are no indications whatever of such an operation's being within the chimpanzees' reach, and most investigators assume that they lack this ability. This lack may be the chief difference between chimpanzee and human intellect.

Koehler introduced the term *insight* (*Einsicht*) for the intellectual operations accessible to chimpanzees. The choice of term is not accidental. Kafka pointed out that Koehler seems to mean by it primarily *seeing* in the literal sense and only by extension "seeing" of relations generally, or comprehension as opposed to blind action [*17*, p. 130].

It must be said that Koehler never defines *insight* or spells out its theory. In the absence of theoretical interpretation, the term is somewhat ambiguous in its application: Sometimes it denotes the specific characteristics of the operation itself, the structure of the chimpanzees' actions; and sometimes it indicates the psychological process preceding and preparing these actions, an internal "plan of operations," as it were. Koehler advances no hypothesis about the mechanism of the intellectual reaction, but it is clear that however it functions and wherever we locate the intellect — in the actions themselves of the chimpanzee or in some preparatory internal process (cerebral or muscular-innervational) — the thesis remains valid that this reaction is determined, not by memory traces, but by the situation as visually presented. Even the best tool for a given problem is lost on the chimpanzee if he cannot see it simultaneously or quasi-simultaneously with the goal.* Thus the consideration of "insight" does not change our conclusion that the chimpanzee, even if he possessed the parrot's gifts, would be exceedingly unlikely to conquer speech.

Yet, as we have said, the chimpanzee has a fairly rich language

* By "quasi-simultaneous perception" Koehler means instances when tool and goal had been seen together a moment earlier, or when they had been used together so many times in an identical situation that they are to all intents and purposes simultaneously perceived psychologically [*18*, p. 39].

of his own. Yerkes's collaborator Learned compiled a dictionary of thirty-two speech elements, or "words," which not only resemble human speech phonetically but also have some meaning, in the sense that they are elicited by certain situations or objects connected with pleasure or displeasure, or inspiring desire, malice, fear [58, p. 54]. These "words" were written down while the apes were waiting to be fed and during meals, in the presence of humans and when two chimpanzees were alone. They are affective vocal reactions, more or less differentiated and to some degree connected, in a conditioned-reflex fashion, with stimuli related to feeding or other vital situations: a strictly emotional language.

In connection with this description of ape speech, we should like to make three points: First, the coincidence of sound production with affective gestures, especially noticeable when the chimpanzees are very excited, is not limited to anthropoids — it is, on the contrary, very common among animals endowed with voice. Human speech certainly originated in the same kind of expressive vocal reactions.

Second, the affective states producing abundant vocal reactions in chimpanzees are unfavorable to the functioning of the intellect. Koehler mentions repeatedly that in chimpanzees, emotional reactions, particularly those of great intensity, rule out a simultaneous intellectual operation.

Third, it must be stressed again that emotional release as such is not the only function of speech in apes. As in other animals and in man, it is also a means of psychological contact with others of their kind. Both in the chimpanzees of Yerkes and Learned and in the apes observed by Koehler, this function of speech is unmistakable. But it is not connected with intellectual reactions, i.e., with thinking. It originates in emotion and is clearly a part of the total emotional syndrome, but a part that fulfills a specific function, both biologically and psychologically. It is far removed from intentional, conscious attempts to inform or influence others. In essence, it is an instinctive reaction, or something extremely close to it.

There can hardly be any doubt that biologically this function of speech is one of the oldest and is genetically related to the visual and vocal signals given by leaders of animal groups. In a recently published study of the language of bees, K. v. Frisch describes very interesting and theoretically important forms of behavior that serve interchange or contact [10] and indubitably originate in instinct. In spite of the phenotypical differences, these behavioral manifestations are basically similar to the speech interchange of chimpanzees. This similarity points up once more the independence of chimpanzee "communications" from any intellectual activity.

We undertook this analysis of several studies of ape language and intellect to elucidate the relationship between thinking and speech in the phylogenetic development of these functions. We can now summarize our conclusions, which will be of use in the further analysis of the problem.

1. Thought and speech have different genetic roots.

2. The two functions develop along different lines and independently of each other.

3. There is no clear-cut and constant correlation between them.

4. Anthropoids display an intellect somewhat like man's *in certain respects* (the embryonic use of tools) and a language somewhat like man's *in totally different respects* (the phonetic aspect of their speech, its release function, the beginnings of a social function).

5. The close correspondence between thought and speech characteristic of man is absent in anthropoids.

6. In the phylogeny of thought and speech, a prelinguistic phase in the development of thought and a preintellectual phase in the development of speech are clearly discernible.

II

Ontogenetically, the relation between thought and speech development is much more intricate and obscure; but here, too, we can distinguish two separate lines springing from two different genetic roots.

The existence of a prespeech phase of thought development in childhood has only recently been corroborated by objective proof. Koehler's experiments with chimpanzees, suitably modified, were carried out on children who had not yet learned to speak. Koehler himself occasionally experimented with children for purposes of comparison, and Buehler undertook a systematic study of a child on the same lines. The findings were similar for children and for apes.

The child's actions, Buehler tells us,

> were exactly like those of the chimpanzees, so that this phase of child life could rather aptly be called the *chimpanzoid age;* in our subject it corresponded to the 10th, 11th, and 12th months. . . . At the chimpanzoid age occur the child's first inventions — very primitive ones to be sure, but extremely important for his mental development [7, p. 46].

What is most important theoretically in these as well as in the chimpanzee experiments is the discovery of the independence of the rudimentary intellectual reactions from speech. Noting this, Buehler comments:

> It used to be said that speech was the beginning of hominization [*Menschwerden*]; maybe so, but before speech there is the thinking involved in the use of tools, i.e., comprehension of mechanical connections, and devising of mechanical means to mechanical ends, or, to put it more briefly still, before speech appears action becomes subjectively meaningful — in other words, consciously purposeful [7, p. 48].

The preintellectual roots of speech in child development have long been known. The child's babbling, crying, even his first words, are quite clearly stages of speech development that have nothing to do with the development of thinking. These manifestations have been generally regarded as a predominantly emotional form of behavior. Not all of them, however, serve merely the function of release. Recent investigations of the earliest forms of behavior in the child and of the child's first reactions to the human voice (by Charlotte Buehler and her circle) have shown that the social function of speech is already clearly apparent during the first year, i.e., in the preintellectual stage of speech development. Quite definite reactions to the human voice were observed as early as during the third week of life, and the first specifically social reaction to voice during the second month [*5*, p. 124]. These investigations also established that laughter, inarticulate sounds, movements, etc., are means of social contact from the first months of the child's life.

Thus the two functions of speech that we observed in phylogenetic development are already present and obvious in the child less than one year old.

But the most important discovery is that at a certain moment at about the age of two the curves of development of thought and speech, till then separate, meet and join to initiate a new form of behavior. Stern's account of this momentous event was the first and the best. He showed how the will to conquer language follows the first dim realization of the purpose of speech, when the child "makes the greatest discovery of his life," that "each thing has its name" [*40*, p. 108].

This crucial instant, when speech begins to serve intellect, and thoughts begin to be spoken, is indicated by two unmistakable objective symptoms: (1) the child's sudden, active curiosity about words, his question about every new thing, "What is this?" and (2) the resulting rapid, saccadic increases in his vocabulary.

Before the turning point, the child does (like some animals) recognize a small number of words which substitute, as in conditioning, for objects, persons, actions, states, or desires. At that age the child knows only the words supplied to him by other people. Now the situation changes: The child feels the need for words and, through his questions, actively tries to learn the signs attached to objects. He seems to have discovered the symbolic function of words. Speech, which in the earlier stage was affective-conative, now enters the intellectual phase. The lines of speech and thought development have met.

At this point the knot is tied for the problem of thought and language. Let us stop and consider exactly what it is that happens when the child makes his "greatest discovery," and whether Stern's interpretation is correct.

Buehler and Koffka both compare this discovery to the chimpanzees' inventions. According to Koffka the name, once discovered by the child, enters into the structure of the object, just as the stick becomes part of the situation of wanting to get the fruit [20, p. 243].

We shall discuss the soundness of this analogy later, when we examine the functional and structural relationships between thought and speech. For the present, we will merely note that the "greatest discovery of the child" becomes possible only when a certain relatively high level of thought and speech development has been reached. In other words, speech cannot be "discovered" without thinking.

In brief, we must conclude that:

1. In their ontogenetic development, thought and speech have different roots.

2. In the speech development of the child, we can with certainty establish a preintellectual stage, and in his thought development, a prelinguistic stage.

3. Up to a certain point in time, the two follow different lines, independently of each other.

4. At a certain point these lines meet, whereupon thought becomes verbal and speech rational.

III

No matter how we approach the controversial problem of the relationship between thought and speech, we shall have to deal extensively with *inner speech*. Its importance in all our thinking is so great that many psychologists, Watson among others, even identify it with thought — which they regard as inhibited, soundless speech. But psychology still does not know how the change from overt to inner speech is accomplished, or at what age, by what process, and why it takes place.

Watson says that we do not know at what point of their speech organization children pass from overt to whispered and then to inner speech because that problem has been studied only incidentally. Our own researches lead us to believe that Watson poses the problem incorrectly. There are no valid reasons to assume that inner speech develops in some mechanical way through a gradual decrease in the audibility of speech (whispering).

It is true that Watson mentions another possibility: "Perhaps," he says, "all three forms develop simultaneously" [54, p. 322]. This hypothesis seems to us as unfounded from the genetic point of view as the sequence: loud speech, whisper, inner speech. No objective data reinforce that *perhaps*. Against it testify the profound dissimilarities between external and inner speech, acknowledged by all psychologists including Watson. There are no grounds for assuming that the two processes, so different *functionally* (social as opposed to personal adaptation) and *structurally* (the extreme, elliptical economy of inner speech, changing the speech pattern almost beyond recognition), may be *genetically* parallel and concurrent. Nor (to return to Watson's main thesis) does it seem plausible that they are linked together by whispered speech, which neither in function nor in structure can be considered a transitional stage between external and inner speech. It stands between the two only phenotypically, not genotypically.

Our studies of whispering in young children fully substantiate this. We have found that structurally there is almost no difference between whispering and speaking aloud; functionally, whispering differs profoundly from inner speech and does not even manifest a tendency toward the characteristics typical of the latter. Furthermore, it does not develop spontaneously until school age, though it may be induced very early: Under social pressure, a three-year-old may, for short periods and with great effort, lower his voice or whisper. This is the one point that may seem to support Watson's view.

While disagreeing with Watson's thesis, we believe that he has hit on the right methodological approach: To solve the problem, we must look for the intermediate link between overt and inner speech.

We are inclined to see that link in the child's egocentric speech, described by Piaget, which, besides its role of accompaniment to activity and its expressive and release functions, readily assumes a planning function, i.e., turns into thought proper quite naturally and easily.

If our hypothesis proves to be correct, we shall have to conclude that speech is interiorized psychologically before it is interiorized physically. Egocentric speech is inner speech in its functions; it is speech on its way inward, intimately tied up with the ordering of the child's behavior, already partly incomprehensible to others, yet still overt in form and showing no tendency to change into whispering or any other sort of half-soundless speech.

We should then also have the answer to the question of *why* speech turns inward. It turns inward because its function changes. Its development would still have three stages — not the ones Watson found, but these: external speech, egocentric speech, inner speech. We should also have at our disposal an excellent method for studying inner speech "live," as it were, while its structural and functional peculiarities are being shaped; it would be an objective method since these peculiarities appear while speech is still audible, i.e., accessible to observation and measurement.

Our investigations show that speech development follows the same course and obeys the same laws as the development of all the other mental operations involving the use of signs, such as counting or mnemonic memorizing. We found that these operations generally develop in four stages. The first is the primitive or natural stage, corresponding to preintellectual speech and preverbal thought, when these operations appear in their original form, as they were evolved at the primitive level of behavior.

Next comes the stage which we might call "naïve psychology," by analogy with what is called "naïve physics" — the child's experience with the physical properties of his own body and of the objects around him, and the application of this experience to the use of tools: the first exercise of the child's budding practical intelligence.

This phase is very clearly defined in the speech development of the child. It is manifested by the correct use of grammatical forms and structures before the child has understood the logical operations for which they stand. The child may operate with subordinate clauses, with words like *because, if, when,* and *but,* long before he really grasps causal, conditional, or temporal relations. He masters syntax of speech before syntax of thought. Piaget's studies proved that grammar develops before logic and that the child learns relatively late the mental operations corresponding to the verbal forms he has been using for a long time.

With the gradual accumulation of naïve psychological experience, the child enters a third stage, distinguished by external signs, external operations that are used as aids in the solution of internal problems. That is the stage when the child counts on his fingers, resorts to mnemonic aids, and so on. In speech development it is characterized by egocentric speech.

The fourth stage we call the "ingrowth" stage. The external operation turns inward and undergoes a profound change in the process. The child begins to count in his head, to use "logical memory," that is, to operate with inherent relationships and inner signs. In speech development this is the final stage of inner, soundless speech. There remains a constant interaction between outer and inner operations, one form effortlessly and frequently changing into the other and back again. Inner speech may come very close in form to external speech or even become exactly like it when it serves as preparation for external speech — for instance, in thinking over a lecture to be given. There is no sharp division between inner and external behavior, and each influences the other.

In considering the function of inner speech in adults after the development is completed, we must ask whether in their case thought and linguistic processes are necessarily connected, whether the two can be equated. Again, as in the case of animals and of children, we must answer "No."

Schematically, we may imagine thought and speech as two intersecting circles. In their overlapping parts, thought and speech coincide to produce what is called verbal thought. Verbal thought, however, does not by any means include all forms of thought or all forms of speech. There is a vast area of thought that has no direct relation to speech. The thinking manifested in the use of tools belongs in this area, as does practical intellect in general. Furthermore, investigations by psychologists of the Wuerzburg school have demonstrated that thought can function without any word images or speech movements detectable through self-observation. The latest experiments show also that there is no direct correspondence between inner speech and the subject's tongue or larynx movements.

Nor are there any psychological reasons to derive all forms of speech activity from thought. No thought process may be involved when a subject silently recites to himself a poem learned by heart or mentally repeats a sentence supplied to him for experimental purposes — Watson notwithstanding. Finally, there is "lyrical" speech prompted by emotion. Though it has all the earmarks of speech, it can scarcely be classified with intellectual activity in the proper sense of the term.

We are therefore forced to conclude that fusion of thought and speech, in adults as well as in children, is a phenomenon limited to a circumscribed area. Nonverbal thought and non-intellectual speech do not participate in this fusion and are affected only indirectly by the processes of verbal thought.

IV

We can now summarize the results of our analysis. We began by attempting to trace the genealogy of thought and speech, using the data of comparative psychology. These data are insufficient for tracing the developmental paths of prehuman thought and speech with any degree of certainty. The basic question, whether anthropoids possess the same type of intellect as man, is still controversial. Koehler answers it in the affirmative, others in the negative. But however this problem may be solved by future investigations, one thing is already clear: In the animal world, the path toward humanlike intellect is not the same as the path toward humanlike speech; thought and speech do not spring from one root.

Even those who would deny intellect to chimpanzees cannot deny that the apes possess something *approaching intellect*, that the highest type of habit formation they manifest is embryonic intellect. Their use of tools prefigures human behavior. To Marxists, Koehler's discoveries do not come as a surprise. Marx [27] said long ago that the use and the creation of implements of labor, although present in embryonic form in some species of animals, are a specific characteristic of the human process of labor. The thesis that the roots of human intellect reach down into the animal realm has long been admitted by Marxism; we find its elaboration in Plekhanov [*34*, p. 138]. Engels [*9*] wrote that man and animals have all forms of intellectual activity in common; only the developmental level differs: Animals are able to reason on an elementary level, to analyze (cracking a nut is a beginning of analysis), to experiment when confronted with problems or caught in a difficult situation. Some, e.g. the parrot, not only can learn to speak but can apply words meaningfully in a restricted sense: When begging, he will use words for which he will be rewarded with a tidbit; when teased, he will let loose the choicest invectives in his vocabulary.

It goes without saying that Engels does not credit animals with the ability to think and to speak on the human level, but we need not at this point elaborate on the exact meaning of his statement. Here we merely wish to establish that there are no good reasons to deny the presence in animals of embryonic thought and language of the same type as man's, which develop, again as in man, along separate paths. An animal's ability to express himself vocally is no indication of his mental development.

Let us now summarize the relevant data yielded by recent studies of children. We find that in the child, too, the roots and the developmental course of the intellect differ from those of speech — that initially thought is nonverbal and speech nonintellectual. Stern asserts that at a certain point the two lines of development meet, speech becoming rational and thought verbal. The child "discovers" that "each thing has its name," and begins to ask what each object is called.

Some psychologists [*8*] do not agree with Stern that this first "age of questions" occurs universally and is necessarily symptomatic of any momentous discovery. Koffka takes a stand between Stern's and that of his opponents. Like Buehler, he emphasizes the analogy between the chimpanzee's invention of tools and the child's discovery of the naming function of language, but the scope of this discovery, according to him, is not as wide as Stern assumed. The word, in Koffka's view, becomes a part of the structure of the object on equal terms with its other parts. For a time, it is to the child not a sign but merely one of

the properties of the object, which has to be supplied to make
the structure complete. As Buehler pointed out, each new object presents the child with a problem situation, and he solves
the problem uniformly by naming the object. When he lacks
the word for the new object, he demands it from adults [7, p.
54].

We believe that this view comes closest to the truth. The data
on children's language (supported by anthropological data)
strongly suggest that for a long time the word is to the child a
property, rather than the symbol, of the object; that the child
grasps the external structure word-object earlier than the inner
symbolic structure. We choose this "middle" hypothesis among
the several offered because we find it hard to believe, on the
basis of available data, that a child of eighteen months to two
years is able to "discover" the symbolic function of speech. This
occurs later, and not suddenly but gradually, through a series of
"molecular" changes. The hypothesis we prefer fits in with the
general pattern of development in mastering signs which we
outlined in the preceding section. Even in a child of school age,
the functional use of a new sign is preceded by a period of mastering the external structure of the sign. Correspondingly, only
in the process of operating with words first conceived as properties of objects does the child discover and consolidate their function as signs.

Thus, Stern's thesis of "discovery" calls for reappraisal and
limitation. Its basic tenet, however, remains valid: It is clear
that ontogenetically thought and speech develop along separate
lines and that at a certain point these lines meet. This important fact is now definitely established, no matter how further
studies may settle the details on which psychologists still dis-
agree: whether this meeting occurs at one point or at several
points, as a truly sudden discovery or after long preparation
through practical use and slow functional change, and whether
it takes place at the age of two or at school age.

We shall now summarize our investigation of inner speech.
Here, too, we considered several hypotheses, and we came to the
conclusion that inner speech develops through a slow accumulation of functional and structural changes, that it branches off

from the child's external speech simultaneously with the differentiation of the social and the egocentric functions of speech, and finally that the speech structures mastered by the child become the basic structures of his thinking.

This brings us to another indisputable fact of great importance: Thought development is determined by language, i.e., by the linguistic tools of thought and by the sociocultural experience of the child. Essentially, the development of inner speech depends on outside factors; the development of logic in the child, as Piaget's studies have shown, is a direct function of his socialized speech. The child's intellectual growth is contingent on his mastering the social means of thought, that is, language.

We can now formulate the main conclusions to be drawn from our analysis. If we compare the early development of speech and of intellect — which, as we have seen, develop along separate lines both in animals and in very young children — with the development of inner speech and of verbal thought, we must conclude that the later stage is not a simple continuation of the earlier. *The nature of the development itself changes,* from biological to sociohistorical. Verbal thought is not an innate, natural form of behavior but is determined by a historical-cultural process and has specific properties and laws that cannot be found in the natural forms of thought and speech. Once we acknowledge the historical character of verbal thought, we must consider it subject to all the premises of historical materialism, which are valid for any historical phenomenon in human society. It is only to be expected that on this level the development of behavior will be governed essentially by the general laws of the historical development of human society.

The problem of thought and language thus extends beyond the limits of natural science and becomes the focal problem of historical human psychology, i.e., of social psychology. Consequently, it must be posed in a different way. This second problem presented by the study of thought and speech will be the subject of a separate investigation.

5

An Experimental Study
of Concept Formation

I

UNTIL RECENTLY the student of concept formation was handicapped by the lack of an experimental method that would allow him to observe the inner dynamics of the process.

The traditional methods of studying concepts fall into two groups. Typical of the first group is the so-called method of definition, with its variations. It is used to investigate the already formed concepts of the child through the verbal definition of their contents. Two important drawbacks make this method inadequate for studying the process in depth. In the first place, it deals with the finished product of concept formation, overlooking the dynamics and the development of the process itself. Rather than tapping the child's thinking, it often elicits a mere reproduction of verbal knowledge, of ready-made definitions provided from without. It may be a test of the child's knowledge and experience, or of his linguistic development, rather than a study of an intellectual process in the true sense. In the second place, this method, concentrating on the word, fails to take into account the perception and the mental elaboration of the sensory material that give birth to the concept. The sensory material and the word are both indispensable parts of concept formation. Studying the word separately puts the process on the purely verbal plane, which is uncharacteristic of child thinking. The relation of the concept to reality remains unexplored; the meaning of a given word is approached through another word, and whatever we discover through this operation is not so much a picture of the child's concepts as a record of the relationship in the child's mind between previously formed families of words.

The second group comprises methods used in the study of abstraction. They are concerned with the psychic processes leading to concept formations. The child is required to discover some common trait in a series of discrete impressions, abstracting it from all the other traits with which it is perceptually fused. Methods of this group disregard the role played by the symbol (the word) in concept formation; a simplified setting substitutes a partial process for the complex structure of the total process.

Thus each of the two traditional methods separates the word from the perceptual material and operates with one or the other. A great step forward was made with the creation of a new method that permits the combination of both parts. The new method introduces into the experimental setting nonsense words which at first mean nothing to the subject. It also introduces artificial concepts by attaching each nonsense word to a particular combination of object attributes for which no ready concept and word exist. For instance, in Ach's experiments [1] the word *gatsun* gradually comes to mean "large and heavy"; the word *fal,* "small and light." This method can be used with both children and adults, since the solution of the problem does not presuppose previous experience or knowledge on the part of the subject. It also takes into account that a concept is not an isolated, ossified, changeless formation but an active part of the intellectual process, constantly engaged in serving communication, understanding, and problem-solving. The new method focuses the investigation on the *functional conditions of concept formation.*

Rimat conducted a carefully designed study of concept formation in adolescents, using a variant of this method. His main conclusion was that true concept formation exceeds the capacities of preadolescents and begins only with the onset of puberty. He writes:

We have definitely established that a sharp increase in the child's ability to form, without help, generalized objective concepts manifests itself only at the close of the twelfth year. . . . Thought in concepts, emancipated from perception, puts demands on the child that exceed his mental possibilities before the age of twelve [35, p. 112].

Ach's and Rimat's investigations disprove the view that concept formation is based on associative connections. Ach demonstrated that the existence of associations, however numerous and strong, between verbal symbols and objects is not in itself sufficient for concept formation. His experimental findings did not confirm the old idea that a concept develops through the maximal strengthening of associative connections involving the attributes common to a group of objects, and the weakening of associations involving the attributes in which these objects differ.

Ach's experiments showed that concept formation is a creative, not a mechanical passive, process; that a concept emerges and takes shape in the course of a complex operation aimed at the solution of some problem; and that the mere presence of external conditions favoring a mechanical linking of word and object does not suffice to produce a concept. In his view, the decisive factor in concept formation is the so-called determining tendency.

Before Ach, psychology postulated two basic tendencies governing the flow of our ideas: reproduction through association, and perseveration. The first brings back those images that had been connected in past experience with the one presently occupying the mind. The second is the tendency of every image to return and to penetrate anew into the flow of images. In his earlier investigations, Ach demonstrated that these two tendencies failed to explain purposeful, consciously directed acts of thought. He therefore assumed that such thoughts were regulated by a third tendency, the "determining tendency," set up by the image of the goal. Ach's study of concepts showed that no new concept was ever formed without the regulating effect of the determining tendency created by the experimental task.

According to Ach's schema, concept formation does not follow the model of an associative chain in which one link calls forth the next; it is an aim-directed process, a series of operations that serve as steps toward a final goal. Memorizing words and connecting them with objects does not in itself lead to concept formation; for the process to begin, a problem must arise that cannot be solved otherwise than through the formation of new concepts.

This characterization of the process of concept formation, however, is still insufficient. The experimental task can be understood and taken over by children long before they are twelve, yet they are unable until that age to form new concepts. Ach's own study demonstrated that children differ from adolescents and adults not in the way they comprehend the aim but in the way their minds work to achieve it. D. Usnadze's [44, 45] detailed experimental study of concept formation in preschoolers also showed that a child at that age approaches problems just as the adult does when he operates with concepts but goes about their solution in an entirely different manner. We can only conclude that it is not the goal or the determining tendency but other factors, unexplored by these researchers, that are responsible for the essential difference between the adult's conceptual thinking and the forms of thought characteristic of the young child.

Usnadze points out that, while fully formed concepts appear relatively late, children begin early to use words and with their aid to establish mutual understanding with adults and among themselves. From this he concludes that words take over the function of concepts and may serve as means of communication long before they reach the level of concepts characteristic of fully developed thought.

We are faced, then, with the following state of affairs: A child is able to grasp a problem, and to visualize the goal it sets, at an early stage in his development; because the tasks of understanding and communication are essentially similar for the child and the adult, the child develops functional equivalents of concepts at an extremely early age, but the forms of thought that he uses in dealing with these tasks differ profoundly from the adult's in their composition, structure, and mode of operation. The main question about the process of concept formation — or about any goal-directed activity — is the question of the means by which the operation is accomplished. Work, for instance, is not sufficiently explained by saying that it is prompted by human needs. We must consider as well the use of tools, the mobilization of the appropriate means without which work could not be performed. To explain the higher forms of human behavior, we must uncover the means by which man learns to organize and direct his behavior.

All the higher psychic functions are mediated processes, and signs are the basic means used to master and direct them. The mediating sign is incorporated in their structure as an indispensable, indeed the central, part of the total process. In concept formation, that sign is the *word*, which at first plays the role of means in forming a concept and later becomes its symbol. In Ach's experiments this role of the word is not given sufficient attention. His study, while it has the merit of discrediting once and for all the mechanistic view of concept formation, did not disclose the true nature of the process — genetically, functionally, or structurally. It took the wrong turn with its purely teleological interpretation, which amounts to asserting that the goal itself creates the appropriate activity via the determining tendency — i.e., that the problem carries its own solution.

II

To study the process of concept formation in its several developmental phases, we used the method worked out by one of our collaborators, L. S. Sakharov [*36*]. It might be described as the "method of double stimulation": Two sets of stimuli are presented to the subject, one set as objects of his activity, the other as signs which can serve to organize that activity.*

* Vygotsky does not describe the test in detail. The following description is taken from *Conceptual Thinking in Schizophrenia*, by E. Hanfmann and J. Kasanin [*16*, pp. 9-10]. — *Editor*

The material used in the concept formation tests consists of 22 wooden blocks varying in color, shape, height, and size. There are 5 different colors, 6 different shapes, 2 heights (the tall blocks and the flat blocks), and 2 sizes of the horizontal surface (large and small). On the underside of each figure, which is not seen by the subject, is written one of the four nonsense words: *lag, bik, mur, cev*. Regardless of color

In some important respects this procedure reverses Ach's experiments on concept formation. Ach begins by giving the subject a learning or practice period; he can handle the objects and
read the nonsense words written on each before being told what
the task will be. In our experiments, the problem is put to the
subject from the start and remains the same throughout, but
the clues to solution are introduced stepwise, with each new
turning of a block. We decided on this sequence because we believe that facing the subject with the task is necessary in order
to get the whole process started. The gradual introduction of
the means of solution permits us to study the total process of
concept formation in all its dynamic phases. The formation
of the concept is followed by its transfer to other objects: the
subject is induced to use the new terms in talking about objects
other than the experimental blocks, and to define their meaning
in a generalized fashion.

---

or shape, *lag* is written on all tall large figures, *bik* on all flat large
figures, *mur* on the tall small ones, and *cev* on the flat small ones. At
the beginning of the experiment all blocks, well mixed as to color, size
and shape, are scattered on a table in front of the subject. . . . The
examiner turns up one of the blocks (the "sample"), shows and reads
its name to the subject, and asks him to pick out all the blocks which
he thinks might belong to the same kind. After the subject has done
so . . . the examiner turns up one of the "wrongly" selected blocks,
shows that this is a block of a different kind, and encourages the subject
to continue trying. After each new attempt another of the wrongly
placed blocks is turned up. As the number of the turned blocks increases, the subject by degrees obtains a basis for discovering to which
characteristics of the blocks the nonsense words refer. As soon as he
makes this discovery the . . . words . . . come to stand for definite
kinds of objects (e.g., *lag* for large tall blocks, *bik* for large flat ones), and
new concepts for which the language provides no names are thus built
up. The subject is then able to complete the task of separating the four
kinds of blocks indicated by the nonsense words. Thus the use of concepts has a definite functional value for the performance required by
this test. Whether the subject actually uses conceptual thinking in trying to solve the problem . . . can be inferred from the nature of the
groups he builds and from his procedure in building them: Nearly
every step in his reasoning is reflected in his manipulations of the blocks.
The first attack on the problem; the handling of the sample; the
response to correction; the finding of the solution—all these stages of
the experiment provide data that can serve as indicators of the subject's
level of thinking.

III

In the series of investigations of the process of concept formation begun in our laboratory by Sakharov and completed by us and our associates Kotelova and Pashkovskaja [*48; 49*, p. 70], more than three hundred people were studied — children, adolescents, and adults, including some with pathological disturbances of intellectual and linguistic activities.

The principal findings of our study may be summarized as follows: The development of the processes which eventually result in concept formation begins in earliest childhood, but the intellectual functions that in a specific combination form the psychological basis of the process of concept formation ripen, take shape, and develop only at puberty. Before that age, we find certain intellectual formations that perform functions similar to those of the genuine concepts to come. With regard to their composition, structure, and operation, these functional equivalents of concepts stand in the same relationship to true concepts as the embryo to the fully formed organism. To equate the two is to ignore the lengthy developmental process between the earliest and the final stage.

Concept formation is the result of a complex activity in which all the basic intellectual functions take part. The process cannot, however, be reduced to association, attention, imagery, inference, or determining tendencies. They are all indispensable, but they are insufficient without the use of the sign, or word, as the means by which we direct our mental operations, control their course, and channel them toward the solution of the problem confronting us.

The presence of a problem that demands the formation of concepts cannot in itself be considered the cause of the process, although the tasks with which society faces the youth as he enters the cultural, professional, and civic world of adults undoubtedly are an important factor in the emergence of conceptual thinking. If the environment presents no such tasks to the adolescent, makes no new demands on him, and does not stimulate his intellect by providing a sequence of new goals, his thinking fails to reach the highest stages, or reaches them with great delay.

The cultural task per se, however, does not explain the developmental mechanism itself that results in concept formation. The investigator must aim to understand the intrinsic bonds between the external tasks and the developmental dynamics, and view concept formation as a function of the adolescent's total social and cultural growth, which affects not only the contents but also the method of his thinking. The new significative use of the word, its use *as a means of concept formation,* is the immediate psychological cause of the radical change in the intellectual process that occurs on the threshold of adolescence.

No new elementary function, essentially different from those already present, appears at this age, but all the existing functions are incorporated into a new structure, form a new synthesis, become parts of a new complex whole; the laws governing this whole also determine the destiny of each individual part. Learning to direct one's own mental processes with the aid of words or signs is an integral part of the process of concept formation. The ability to regulate one's actions by using auxiliary means reaches its full development only in adolescence.

IV

Our investigation brought out that the ascent to concept formation is made in three basic phases, each divided in turn into several stages. In this and in the following six sections, we shall describe these phases and their subdivisions as they appear when studied by the method of "double stimulation."

The young child takes the first step toward concept formation when he puts together a number of objects in an *unorganized congeries,* or "heap," in order to solve a problem that we adults would normally solve by forming a new concept. The heap, consisting of disparate objects grouped together without any basis reveals a diffuse, undirected extension of the meaning of the sign (artificial word) to inherently unrelated objects linked by chance in the child's perception.

At that stage, word meaning denotes nothing more to the child than a *vague syncretic conglomeration of individual ob-*

jects that have somehow or other coalesced into an image in his mind. Because of its syncretic origin, that image is highly unstable.

In perception, in thinking, and in acting, the child tends to merge the most diverse elements into one unarticulated image on the strength of some chance impression. Claparède gave the name "syncretism" to this well-known trait of child thought. Blonski called it the "incoherent coherence" of child thinking. We have described the phenomenon elsewhere as the result of a tendency to compensate for the paucity of well-apprehended objective relations by an overabundance of subjective connections and to mistake these subjective bonds for real bonds between things. These syncretic relationships, and the heaps of objects assembled under one word meaning, also reflect objective bonds in so far as the latter coincide with the relations between the child's perceptions or impressions. Many words, therefore, have in part the same meaning to the child and the adult, especially words referring to concrete objects in the child's habitual surroundings. The child's and the adult's meanings of a word often "meet," as it were, in the same concrete object, and this suffices to ensure mutual understanding.

The first phase of concept formation, which we have just outlined, subsumes three distinct stages. We were able to observe them in detail within the framework of the experimental study.

The first stage in the formation of syncretic heaps that represent to the child the meaning of a given artificial word is a manifestation of the *trial-and-error* stage in the development of thinking. The group is created at random, and each object added is a mere guess or trial; it is replaced by another object when the guess is proven wrong, i.e., when the experimenter turns the object and shows that it has a different name.

During the next stage, the composition of the group is determined largely by the spatial position of the experimental objects, i.e., by a purely syncretic *organization of the child's visual field*. The syncretic image or group is formed as a result of the single elements' contiguity in space or in time, or of their being brought into some other more complex relationship by the child's immediate perception.

During the third stage of the first phase of concept formation, the syncretic image rests in a more complex base: It is composed of *elements taken from different groups or heaps that have already been formed by the child in the ways described above.* These newly combined elements have no intrinsic bonds with one another, so that the new formation has the same "incoherent coherence" as the first heaps. The sole difference is that in trying to give meaning to a new word the child now goes through a two-step operation, but this more elaborate operation remains syncretic and results in no more order than the simple assembling of heaps.

V

The second major phase on the way to concept formation comprises many variations of a type of thinking that we shall call *thinking in complexes.* In a complex, individual objects are united in the child's mind not only by his subjective impressions but also by *bonds actually existing between these objects.* This is a new achievement, an ascent to a much higher level.

When the child moves up to that level, he has partly outgrown his egocentrism. He no longer mistakes connections between his own impressions for connections between things — a decisive step away from syncretism toward objective thinking. Thought in complexes is already coherent and objective thinking, although it does not reflect objective relationships in the same way as conceptual thinking.

Remains of complex thinking persist in the language of adults. Family names are perhaps the best example of this. Any family name, "Petrov," let us say, subsumes individuals in a manner closely resembling that of the child's complexes. The child at that stage of development thinks in family names, as it were; the universe of individual objects becomes organized for him by being grouped into separate, mutually related "families."

In a complex, the bonds between its components are *concrete and factual* rather than abstract and logical, just as we do not classify a person as belonging to the Petrov family because of any logical relationship between him and other bearers of the name. The question is settled for us by facts.

The factual bonds underlying complexes are discovered through direct experience. A complex therefore is first and foremost a concrete grouping of objects connected by factual bonds. Since a complex is not formed on the plane of abstract logical thinking, the bonds that create it, as well as the bonds it helps to create, lack logical unity; they may be of many different kinds. *Any factually present* connection may lead to the inclusion of a given element into a complex. That is the main difference between a complex and a concept. While a concept groups objects according to one attribute, the bonds relating the elements of a complex to the whole and to one another may be as diverse as the contacts and relationships of the elements are in reality.

In our investigation we observed five basic types of complexes, which succeed one another during this stage of development.

We call the first type of complex the *associative type*. It may be based on any bond the child notices between the sample object and some other blocks. In our experiment, the sample object, the one first given to the subject with its name visible, forms the nucleus of the group to be built. In building an associative complex, the child may add one block to the nuclear object because it is of the same color, another because it is similar to the nucleus in shape or in size, or in any other attribute that happens to strike him. Any bond between the nucleus and another object suffices to make the child include that object in the group and to designate it by the common "family name." The bond between the nucleus and the other object need not be a common trait, such as the same color or shape; a similarity, or a contrast, or proximity in space may also establish the bond.

To the child at that stage the word ceases to be the "proper name" of an individual object; it becomes the family name of a group of objects related to one another in many kinds of ways, just as the relationships in human families are many and different.

VI

Complex thinking of the second type consists in combining objects or the concrete impressions they make on the child into groups that most closely resemble *collections*. Objects are placed together on the basis of some one trait in which they differ and consequently complement one another.

In our experiments the child would pick out objects differing from the sample in color, or in form, or in size, or in some other characteristic. He did not pick them at random; he chose them because they contrasted with and complemented the one attribute of the sample which he took to be the basis of grouping. The result was a collection of the colors or forms present in the experimental material, e.g. a group of blocks each of a different color.

Association by contrast, rather than by similarity, guides the child in compiling a collection. This form of thinking, however, is often combined with the associative form proper, described earlier, producing a collection based on mixed principles. The child fails to adhere throughout the process to the principle he originally accepted as the basis of collecting. He slips into the consideration of a different trait, so that the resulting group becomes a mixed collection, e.g., of both colors and shapes.

This long, persistent stage in the development of child thinking is rooted in his practical experience, in which collections of complementary things often form a set or a whole. Experience teaches the child certain forms of functional grouping: cup, saucer, and spoon; a place setting of knife, fork, spoon, and plate; the set of clothes he wears. All these are models of natural collection complexes. Even adults, when speaking of dishes or clothes, usually have in mind sets of concrete objects rather than generalized concepts.

To recapitulate, the syncretic image leading to the formation of "heaps" is based on vague subjective bonds mistaken for actual bonds between objects; the associative complex, on similarities or other perceptually compelling ties between things; the collection complex, on relationships between objects observed in practical experience. We might say that the collection complex is a *grouping of objects on the basis of their participation in the same practical operation* — of their functional co-operation.

VII

After the collection stage of thinking in complexes, we must place the *chain complex* — a dynamic, consecutive joining of individual links into a single chain, with meaning carried over from one link to the next. For instance, if the experimental sample is a yellow triangle, the child might pick out a few triangular blocks until his attention is caught by, let us say, the blue color of a block he has just added; he switches to selecting blue blocks of any shape — angular, circular, semicircular. This in turn is sufficient to change the criterion again; oblivious of color, the child begins to choose rounded blocks. The decisive attribute keeps changing during the entire process. There is no consistency in the type of the bonds or in the manner in which a link of the chain is joined with the one that precedes and the one that follows it. The original sample has no central significance. Each link, once included in a chain complex, is as important as the first and may become the magnet for a series of other objects.

The chain formation strikingly demonstrates the perceptually concrete, factual nature of complex thinking. An object included because of one of its attributes enters the complex not just as the carrier of that one trait but as an individual, with *all* its attributes. The single trait is not abstracted by the child from the rest and is not given a special role, as in a concept. In complexes, the hierarchical organization is absent: All attributes are functionally equal. The sample may be disregarded altogether when a bond is formed between two other objects; these objects may have nothing in common with some of the other elements either, and yet be parts of the same chain on the strength of sharing an attribute with still another of its elements.

Therefore, the chain complex may be considered the *purest form of thinking in complexes*. Unlike the associative complex, whose elements are, after all, interconnected through one element — the nucleus of the complex — the chain complex has no nucleus; there are relations between single elements, but nothing more.

A complex does not rise above its elements as does a concept; it merges with the concrete objects that compose it. This fusion of the general and the particular, of the complex and its elements, this psychic amalgam, as Werner called it, is the distinctive characteristic of all complex thinking and of the chain complex in particular.

VIII

Because the chain complex is factually inseparable from the group of concrete objects that form it, it often acquires a vague and floating quality. The type and nature of the bonds may change from link to link almost imperceptibly. Often a remote similarity is enough to create a bond. Attributes are sometimes considered similar, not because of genuine likeness, but because of a dim impression that they have something in common. This leads to the fourth type of complex observed in our experiments. It might be called the diffuse complex.

The *diffuse complex* is marked by the fluidity of the very attribute that unites its single elements. Perceptually concrete groups of objects or images are formed by means of diffuse, indeterminate bonds. To go with a yellow triangle, for example, a child would in our experiments pick out trapezoids as well as triangles, because they made him think of triangles with their tops cut off. Trapezoids would lead to squares, squares to hexagons, hexagons to semicircles, and finally to circles. Color as the basis of selection is equally floating and changeable. Yellow objects are apt to be followed by green ones; then green may change to blue, and blue to black.

Complexes resulting from this kind of thinking are so indefinite as to be in fact limitless. Like a Biblical tribe that longed to multiply until it became countless like the stars in the sky or the sands of the sea, a diffuse complex in the child's mind is a kind of family that has limitless powers to expand by adding more and more individuals to the original group.

The child's generalizations in the nonpractical and nonperceptual areas of his thinking, which cannot be easily verified through perception or practical action, are the real-life parallel of the diffuse complexes observed in the experiments. It is well known that the child is capable of surprising transitions, of startling associations and generalizations, when his thought ventures beyond the boundaries of the small tangible world of his experience. Outside it he often constructs limitless complexes amazing in the universality of the bonds they encompass.

These limitless complexes, however, are built on the same principles as the circumscribed concrete complexes. In both, the child stays within the limits of concrete bonds between things, but in so far as the first kind of complex comprises objects outside the sphere of his practical cognition, these bonds are naturally based on dim, unreal, unstable attributes.

IX

To complete the picture of complex thinking, we must describe one more type of complex — the bridge, as it were, between complexes and the final, highest stage in the development of concept formation.

We call this type of complex the *pseudo-concept* because the generalization formed in the child's mind, although phenotypically resembling the adult concept, is psychologically very different from the concept proper; in its essence, it is still a complex.

In the experimental setting, the child produces a pseudo-concept every time he surrounds a sample with objects that could just as well have been assembled on the basis of an abstract concept. For instance, when the sample is a yellow triangle and the child picks out all the triangles in the experimental material, he could have been guided by the general idea or concept of a triangle. Experimental analysis shows, however, that in reality the child is guided by the concrete, visible likeness and has formed only an associative complex limited to a certain kind of perceptual bond. Although the results are identical, the process by which they are reached is not at all the same as in conceptual thinking.*

* The following elaboration of the experimental observations is taken from the study by E. Hanfmann and J. Kasanin [*16*, pp. 30-31]:

> In many cases the group, or groups, created by the subject have quite the same appearance as in a consistent classification, and the lack of a true conceptual foundation is not revealed until the subject is required to put in operation the ideas that underlie this grouping. This happens

We must consider this type of complex in some detail. It plays a predominant role in the child's real-life thinking, and it is important as a transitional link between thinking in complexes and true concept formation.

X

Pseudo-concepts predominate over all other complexes in the preschool child's thinking for the simple reason that in real life *complexes corresponding to word meanings are not spontaneously developed by the child: The lines along which a complex develops are predetermined by the meaning a given word already has in the language of adults.*

In our experiments, the child, freed from the directing influence of familiar words, was able to develop word meanings and form complexes according to his own preferences. Only through the experiment can we gauge the kind and extent of his spontaneous activity in mastering the language of adults. The child's own activity in forming generalizations is by no means quenched, though it is usually hidden from view and driven into complicated channels by the influences of adult speech.

---

at the moment of correction when the examiner turns one of the wrongly selected blocks and shows that the word written on it is different from the one on the sample block, e.g. that it is not *mur*. This is one of the critical points of the experiment. . . .

Subjects who have approached the task as a classification problem respond to correction immediately in a perfectly specific way. This response is adequately expressed in the statement: "Aha! Then it is not color" (or shape, etc.). . . . The subject removes all the blocks he had placed with the sample one, and starts looking for another possible classification.

On the other hand, the outward behavior of the subject at the beginning of the experiment may have been that of attempting a classification. He may have placed all red blocks with the sample, proceeding quite consistently . . . and declared that he thinks those red blocks are the *murs*. Now the examiner turns up one of the chosen blocks and shows that it has a different name. . . . The subject sees it removed or even obediently removes it himself, but that is all he does: he makes no attempt to remove the other red blocks from the sample *mur*. To the examiner's question if he still thinks that those blocks belong together, and are *mur*, he answers definitely, "Yes, they still belong together because they are red." This striking reply betrays an attitude totally incompatible with a true classification approach and proves that the groups he had formed were actually pseudo-classes.

The language of the environment, with its stable, permanent meanings, points the way that the child's generalizations will take. But, constrained as it is, the child's thinking proceeds along this preordained path in the manner peculiar to his level of intellectual development. The adult cannot pass on to the child his mode of thinking. He merely supplies the ready-made meaning of a word, around which the child forms a complex — with all the structural, functional, and genetic peculiarities of thinking in complexes, even if the product of his thinking is in fact identical in its content with a generalization that could have been formed by conceptual thinking. The outward similarity between the pseudo-concept and the real concept, which makes it very difficult to "unmask" this kind of complex, is a major obstacle in the genetic analysis of thought.

The functional equivalence of complex and concept, the coincidence, in practice, of many word meanings for the adult and the three-year-old child, the possibility of mutual understanding, and the apparent similarity of their thought processes have led to the false assumption that all the forms of adult intellectual activity are already present in embryo in child thinking and that no drastic change occurs at the age of puberty. It is easy to understand the origin of that misconception. The child learns very early a large number of words that mean the same to him and to the adult. The mutual understanding of adult and child creates the illusion that the end point in the development of word meaning coincides with the starting point, that the concept is provided ready-made from the beginning, and that no development takes place.

The child's acquisition of the language of adults accounts, in fact, for the consonance of his complexes with their concepts — in other words, for the emergence of concept complexes, or pseudo-concepts. Our experiments, in which the child's thinking is not hemmed in by word meanings, demonstrate that if it were not for the prevalence of pseudo-concepts the child's complexes would develop along different lines from adult concepts, and verbal communication between children and adults would be impossible.

The pseudo-concept serves as the connecting link between

thinking in complexes and thinking in concepts. It is dual in nature: a complex already carrying the germinating seed of a concept. Verbal intercourse with adults thus becomes a powerful factor in the development of the child's concepts. The transition from thinking in complexes to thinking in concepts passes unnoticed by the child because his pseudo-concepts already coincide in content with the adult's concepts. Thus the child begins to operate with concepts, to practice conceptual thinking, before he is clearly aware of the nature of these operations. This peculiar genetic situation is not limited to the attainment of concepts; it is the rule rather than an exception in the intellectual development of the child.

XI

We have now seen, with the clarity that only experimental analysis can give, the various stages and forms of complex thinking. This analysis permits us to uncover the very essence of the genetic process of concept formation in a schematic form, and thus gives us the key to the understanding of the process as it unfolds in real life. But an experimentally induced process of concept formation never mirrors the genetic development exactly as it occurs in life. The basic forms of concrete thinking that we have enumerated appear in reality in mixed states. The morphological analysis given so far must be followed by a functional and genetic analysis. We must try to connect the forms of complex thinking discovered in the experiment with the forms of thought found in the actual development of the child and check the two series of observations against each other.

From our experiments we concluded that, at the complex stage, word meanings as perceived by the child refer to the same objects the adult has in mind, which ensures understanding between child and adult, but that the child thinks the same thing in a different way, by means of different mental operations. We shall try to verify this proposition by comparing our observations with the data on the peculiarities of child thought, and of primitive thought in general, previously collected by psychological science.

If we observe what groups of objects the child links together in transferring the meanings of his first words, and how he goes about it, we discover a mixture of the two forms which we called in our experiments the associative complex and the syncretic image.

Let us borrow an illustration from Idelberger, cited by Werner [55, p. 206]. On the 251st day of his life, a child applies the word *bow-wow* to a china figurine of a girl that usually stands on the sideboard and that he likes to play with. On the 307th day, he applies *bow-wow* to a dog barking in the yard, to the pictures of his grandparents, to a toy dog, and to a clock. On the 331st day, to a fur piece with an animal's head, noticing particularly the glass eyes, and to another fur stole without a head. On the 334th day, to a rubber doll that squeaks when pressed, and on the 396th, to his father's cuff links. On the 433rd day, he utters the same word at the sight of pearl buttons on a dress and of a bath thermometer.

Werner analyzed this example and concluded that the diverse things called *bow-wow* may be catalogued as follows: first, dogs and toy dogs, and small oblong objects resembling the china doll, e.g. the rubber doll and the thermometer; second, the cuff links, pearl buttons, and similar small objects. The criterial attribute is an oblong shape or a shiny surface resembling eyes.

Clearly, the child unites these concrete objects according to the principle of a complex. Such spontaneous complex formations make up the entire first chapter of the developmental history of children's words.

There is a well-known, frequently cited example of these shifts: a child's use of *quah* to designate first a duck swimming in a pond, then any liquid, including the milk in his bottle; when he happens to see a coin with an eagle on it, the coin also is called *quah,* and then any round, coinlike object. This is a typical chain complex: Each new object included has some attribute in common with another element, but the attributes undergo endless changes.

Complex formation is also responsible for the peculiar phenomenon that one word may in different situations have different or even opposite meanings as long as there is some associative link between them. Thus, a child may say *before* for both before and after, or *tomorrow* for both tomorrow and yesterday. We have here a perfect analogy with some ancient languages — Hebrew, Chinese, Latin — in which one word also sometimes indicated opposites. The Romans, for instance, had one word for high and deep. Such a marriage of opposite meanings is possible only as a result of thinking in complexes.

XII

There is another very interesting trait of primitive thought that shows us complex thinking in action and points up the difference between pseudo-concepts and concepts. This trait — which Levy-Bruhl was the first to note in primitive peoples, Storch in the insane, and Piaget in children — is usually called *participation.* The term is applied to the relationship of partial identity or close interdependence established by primitive thought between two objects or phenomena which actually have neither contiguity nor any other recognizable connection.

Levy-Bruhl [26] quotes von den Steinen regarding a striking case of participation observed among the Bororo of Brazil, who pride themselves on being red parrots. Von den Steinen at first did not know what to make of such a categorical assertion but finally decided that they really meant it. It was not merely a name they appropriated, or a family relationship they insisted upon: What they meant was identity of beings.

It seems to us that the phenomenon of participation has not yet received a sufficiently convincing psychological explanation, and this for two reasons: First, investigations have tended to focus on the contents of the phenomenon and to ignore the mental operations involved, i.e., to study the product rather than the process; second, no adequate attempts have been made to view the phenomenon in the context of the other bonds and relationships formed by the primitive mind. Too often the extreme, the fantastic, like the Bororo notion that they are red parrots, attracts investigation at the expense of less spectacular phenomena. Yet careful analysis shows that even those connections that do not outwardly clash with our logic are formed by the primitive mind on the principles of complex thinking.

Since children of a certain age think in pseudo-concepts, and words designate to them complexes of concrete objects, their thinking must result in participation, i.e., in bonds unacceptable to adult logic. A particular thing may be included in different complexes on the strength of its different concrete attributes and consequently may have several names; which one is used depends on the complex activated at the time. In our experiments, we frequently observed instances of this kind of participation where an object was included simultaneously in two or more complexes. Far from being an exception, participation is characteristic of complex thinking.

Primitive peoples also think in complexes, and consequently the word in their languages does not function as the carrier of a concept but as a "family name" for groups of concrete objects belonging together, not logically, but factually. Storch has shown that the same kind of thinking is characteristic of schizophrenics, who regress from conceptual thought to a more primitive level of mentation, rich in images and symbols. He considers the use of concrete images instead of abstract concepts one of the most distinctive traits of primitive thought. Thus the child, primitive man, and the insane, much as their thought processes may differ in other important respects, all manifest participation — a symptom of primitive complex thinking and of the function of words as family names.

We therefore believe that Levy-Bruhl's way of interpreting participation is incorrect. He approaches the Bororo statements about being red parrots from the point of view of our own logic when he assumes that to the primitive mind, too, such an assertion means identity of beings. But since words to the Bororo designate groups of objects, not concepts, their assertion has a different meaning: The word for parrot is the word for a complex that includes parrots and themselves. It does not imply identity any more than a family name shared by two related individuals implies that they are one and the same person.

XIII

The history of language clearly shows that complex thinking with all its peculiarities is the very foundation of linguistic development.

Modern linguistics distinguishes between the meaning of a word, or an expression, and its referent, i.e., the object it designates. There may be one meaning and different referents, or different meanings and one referent. Whether we say "the victor at Jena" or "the loser at Waterloo," we refer to the same person, yet the meaning of the two phrases differs. There is but one category of words — proper names — whose sole function is that of reference. Using this terminology, we might say that the child's and the adult's words coincide in their referents but not in their meanings.

Identity of referent combined with divergence of meaning is also found in the history of languages. A multitude of facts support this thesis. The synonyms existing in every language are one good example. The Russian language has two words for moon, arrived at by different thought processes that are clearly reflected in their etymology. One term derives from the Latin word connoting "caprice, inconstancy, fancy." It was obviously meant to stress the changing form that distinguishes the moon from the other celestial bodies. The originator of the second term, which means "measurer," had no doubt been impressed by the fact that time could be measured by lunar phases. Between languages, the same holds true. For instance, in Russian the word for tailor stems from an old word for a piece of cloth; in French and in German it means "one who cuts."

If we trace the history of a word in any language, we shall see, however surprising this may seem at first blush, that its meanings change just as in child thinking. In the example we have cited, *bow-wow* was applied to a series of objects totally disparate from the adult point of view. Similar transfers of meaning, indicative of complex thinking, are the rule rather than the exception in the development of a language. Russian has a term for day-and-night, the word *sutki*. Originally it meant a seam, the junction of two pieces of cloth, something woven together; then it was used for any junction, e.g. of two walls of a house, and hence a corner; it began to be used metaphorically for twilight, "where day and night meet"; then it came to mean the time from one twilight to the next, i.e., the 24-hour *sutki* of the present. Such diverse things as a seam, a corner, twilight, and

24 hours are drawn into one complex in the course of the development of a word, in the same way as the child incorporates different things into a group on the basis of concrete imagery.

What are the laws governing the formation of word families? More often than not, new phenomena or objects are named after unessential attributes, so that the name does not truly express the nature of the thing named. Because a name is never a concept when it first emerges, it is usually both too narrow and too broad. For instance, the Russian word for cow originally meant "horned," and the word for mouse, "thief." But there is much more to a cow than horns, and to a mouse than pilfering; thus their names are too narrow. On the other hand, they are too broad, since the same epithets may be applied — and actually are applied in some other languages — to a number of other creatures. The result is a ceaseless struggle within the developing language between conceptual thought and the heritage of primitive thinking in complexes. The complex-created name, based on one attribute, conflicts with the concept for which it has come to stand. In the contest between the concept and the image that gave birth to the name, the image gradually loses out; it fades from consciousness and from memory, and the original meaning of the word is eventually obliterated. Years ago all ink was black, and the Russian word for ink refers to its blackness. This does not prevent us today from speaking of red, green, or blue "blacking" without noticing the incongruity of the combination.

Transfers of names to new objects occur through contiguity or similarity, i.e., on the basis of concrete bonds typical of thinking in complexes. Words in the making in our own era present many examples of the process by which miscellaneous things are grouped together. When we speak of "the leg of a table," "the elbow of a road," "the neck of a bottle," and "a bottleneck," we are grouping things in a complexlike fashion. In these cases the visual and functional similarities mediating the transfer are quite clear. Transfer can be determined, however, by the most varied associations, and if it has occurred in the remote past, it is impossible to reconstruct the connections without knowing exactly the historical background of the event.

The primary word is not a straightforward symbol for a concept but rather an image, a picture, a mental sketch of a concept, a short tale about it — indeed, a small work of art. In naming an object by means of such a pictorial concept, man ties it into one group with a number of other objects. In this respect the process of language creation is analogous to the process of complex formation in the intellectual development of the child.

XIV

Much can be learned about complex thinking from the speech of deaf-mute children, in whose case the main stimulus to the formation of pseudo-concepts is absent. Deprived of verbal intercourse with adults and left to determine for themselves what objects to group under a common name, they form their complexes freely, and the special characteristics of complex thinking appear in pure, clear-cut form.

In the sign language of deaf-mutes, touching a tooth may have three different meanings: "white," "stone," and "tooth." All three belong to one complex whose further elucidation requires an additional pointing or imitative gesture to indicate the object meant in each case. The two functions of a word are, so to speak, physically separated. A deaf-mute touches his tooth and then, by pointing at its surface or by making a throwing gesture, tells us to what object he refers in a given case.

To test and supplement our experimental results, we have taken some examples of complex formation from the linguistic development of children, the thinking of primitive peoples, and the development of languages as such. It should be noted, however, that even the normal adult, capable of forming and using concepts, does not consistently operate with concepts in his thinking. Apart from the primitive thought processes of dreams, the adult constantly shifts from conceptual to concrete, complexlike thinking. The transitional, pseudo-concept form of thought is not confined to child thinking; we too resort to it very often in our daily life.

XV

Our investigation led us to divide the process of concept formation into three major phases. We have described two of them, marked by the predominance of the syncretic image and of the complex, respectively, and we come now to the third phase. Like the second, it can be subdivided into several stages.

In reality, the new formations do not necessarily appear only after complex thinking has run the full course of its development. In a rudimentary shape, they can be observed long before the child begins to think in pseudo-concepts. Essentially, however, they belong in the third division of our schema of concept formation. If complex thinking is one root of concept formation, the forms we are about to describe are a second, independent root. They have a distinct genetic function, different from that of complexes, in the child's mental development.

The principal function of complexes is to establish bonds and relationships. Complex thinking begins the unification of scattered impressions; by organizing discrete elements of experience into groups, it creates a basis for later generalizations.

But the advanced concept presupposes more than unification. To form such a concept it is also necessary *to abstract, to single out* elements, and to view the abstracted elements apart from the totality of the concrete experience in which they are embedded. In genuine concept formation, it is equally important to unite and to separate: Synthesis must be combined with analysis. Complex thinking cannot do both. Its very essence is overabundance, overproduction of connections, and weakness in abstraction. To fulfill the second requirement is the function of the processes that ripen only during the third phase in the development of concept formation, though their beginnings reach back into much earlier periods.

In our experiment, the first step toward abstraction was made when the child grouped together *maximally similar* objects, e.g. objects that were small *and* round, or red *and* flat. Since the test material contains no identical objects, even the maximally similar are dissimilar in some respects. It follows that in picking out these "best matches" the child must be paying more attention to some traits of an object than to others — giving them preferential treatment, so to speak. The attributes which, added up, make an object maximally similar to the sample become the focus of attention and are thereby, in a sense, abstracted from the attributes to which the child attends less. This first attempt at abstraction is not obvious as such, because the child abstracts a whole group of traits, without clearly distinguishing one from another; often the abstraction of such a group of attributes is based only on a vague, general impression of the objects' similarity.

Still, the global character of the child's perception has been breached. An object's attributes have been divided into two parts unequally attended to — a beginning of positive and negative abstraction. An object no longer enters a complex *in toto*, with all its attributes — some are denied admission; if the object is impoverished thereby, the attributes that caused its inclusion in the complex acquire a sharper relief in the child's thinking.

XVI

During the next stage in the development of abstraction, the grouping of objects on the basis of maximum similarity is superseded by grouping on the basis of a single attribute: e.g., only round objects or only flat ones. Although the product is undistinguishable from the product of a concept, these formations, like pseudo-concepts, are only precursors of true concepts. Following the usage introduced by Groos [*14*], we shall call such formations *potential concepts*.

Potential concepts result from a species of isolating abstraction of such a primitive nature that it is present to some degree not only in very young children but even in animals. Hens can be trained to respond to one distinct attribute in different objects, such as color or shape, if it indicates accessible food; Koehler's chimpanzees, once they had learned to use a stick as a tool, used other long objects when they needed a stick and none was available.

Even in very young children, objects or situations that have some features in common evoke like responses; at the earliest preverbal stage, children clearly expect similar situations to lead to identical outcomes. Once a child has associated a word with an object, he readily applies it to a new object that impresses him as similar in some ways to the first. Potential concepts, then, may be formed either in the sphere of perceptual or in that of practical, action-bound thinking — on the basis of similar impressions in the first case and of similar functional meanings in the second. The latter are an important source of potential concepts. It is well known that until early school age functional meanings play a very important role in child thinking. When asked to explain a word, a child will tell what the object the word designates can do, or — more often — what can be done with it. Even abstract concepts are often translated into the language of concrete action: *"Reasonable* means when I am hot and don't stand in a draft."

Potential concepts already play a part in complex thinking, in so far as abstraction occurs also in complex formation. Associative complexes, for instance, presuppose the "abstraction" of one trait common to different units. But as long as complex thinking predominates, the abstracted trait is unstable, has no privileged position, and easily yields its temporary dominance to other traits. In potential concepts proper, a trait once abstracted is not easily lost again among the other traits. The concrete totality of traits has been destroyed through its abstraction, and the possibility of unifying the traits on a different basis opens up. Only the mastery of abstraction, combined with advanced complex thinking, enables the child to progress to the formation of genuine concepts. A concept emerges only when the abstracted traits are synthesized anew and the resulting abstract synthesis becomes the main instrument of thought. The decisive role in this process, as our experiments have shown, is played by the word, deliberately used to direct all the part processes of advanced concept formation.*

* It must be clear from this chapter that words also fulfill an important, though different, function in the various stages of thinking in complexes. Therefore, we consider complex thinking a stage in the development of *verbal* thinking, unlike many other authors [21, 53, 55] who extend the term *complex* to include preverbal thinking and even the primitive mentation of animals.

XVII

In our experimental study of the intellectual processes of adolescents, we observed how the primitive syncretic and complex forms of thinking gradually subside, potential concepts are used less and less, and true concepts begin to be formed — seldom at first, then with increasing frequency. Even after the adolescent has learned to produce concepts, however, he does not abandon the more elementary forms; they continue for a long time to operate, indeed to predominate, in many areas of his thinking. Adolescence is less a period of completion than one of crisis and transition.

The transitional character of adolescent thinking becomes especially evident when we observe the actual functioning of the newly acquired concepts. Experiments specially devised to study the adolescent's operations with concepts bring out, in the first place, a striking discrepancy between his ability to form concepts and his ability to define them.

The adolescent will form and use a concept quite correctly in a concrete situation but will find it strangely difficult to express that concept in words, and the verbal definition will, in most cases, be much narrower than might have been expected from the way he used the concept. The same discrepancy occurs also in adult thinking, even at very advanced levels. This confirms the assumption that concepts evolve in ways differing from deliberate conscious elaboration of experience in logical terms. Analysis of reality with the help of concepts precedes analysis of the concepts themselves.

The adolescent encounters another obstacle when he tries to apply a concept that he has formed in a specific situation to a new set of objects or circumstances, where the attributes synthesized in the concept appear in configurations differing from the original one. (An example would be the application to everyday objects of the new concept "small and tall," evolved on test blocks.) Still, the adolescent is usually able to achieve such a transfer at a fairly early stage of development.

Much more difficult than the transfer itself is the task of defining a concept when it is no longer rooted in the original situation and must be formulated on a purely abstract plane, without reference to any concrete situation or impressions. In our experiments, the child or adolescent who had solved the problem of concept formation correctly very often descended to a more primitive level of thought in giving a verbal definition of the concept and began simply to enumerate the various objects to which the concept applied in the particular setting. In this case he operated with the name as with a concept but defined it as a complex — a form of thought vacillating between complex and concept, and typical of that transitional age.

The greatest difficulty of all is the application of a concept, finally grasped and formulated on the abstract level, to new concrete situations that must be viewed in these abstract terms — a kind of transfer usually mastered only toward the end of the adolescent period. The transition from the abstract to the concrete proves just as arduous for the youth as the earlier transition from the concrete to the abstract. Our experiments leave no doubt that on this point at any rate the description of concept formation given by traditional psychology, which simply reproduced the schema of formal logic, is totally unrelated to reality.

According to the classical school, concept formation is achieved by the same process as the "family portrait" in Galton's composite photographs. These are made by taking pictures of different members of a family on the same plate, so that the "family" traits common to several people stand out with an extraordinary vividness, while the differing personal traits of individuals are blurred by the superimposition. A similar intensification of traits shared by a number of objects is supposed to occur in concept formation; according to traditional theory, the sum of these traits *is* the concept. In reality, as some psychologists have long ago noted, and as our experiments show, the path by which adolescents arrive at concept formation never conforms to this logical schema. When the process of concept formation is seen in all its complexity, it appears as a *movement* of thought within the pyramid of concepts, constantly alternating between two directions, from the particular to the general, and from the general to the particular.

Our investigation has shown that a concept is formed, not through the interplay of associations, but through an intellectual operation in which all the elementary mental functions participate in a specific combination. This operation is guided by the use of words as the means of actively centering attention, of abstracting certain traits, synthesizing them, and symbolizing them by a sign.

The processes leading to concept formation develop along two main lines. The first is complex formation: The child unites diverse objects in groups under a common "family name"; this process passes through various stages. The second line of development is the formation of "potential concepts," based on singling out certain common attributes. In both, the use of the word is an integral part of the developing processes, and the word maintains its guiding function in the formation of genuine concepts, to which these processes lead.

6

The Development of Scientific Concepts in Childhood

I

To DEVISE successful methods of instructing the schoolchild in systematic knowledge, it is necessary to understand the development of scientific concepts in the child's mind. No less important than this practical aspect of the problem is its theoretical significance for psychological science. Yet our knowledge of the entire subject is surprisingly scanty.

What happens in the mind of the child to the scientific concepts he is taught at school? What is the relationship between the assimilating of information and the internal development of a scientific concept in the child's consciousness?

Contemporary child psychology has two answers to these questions. One school of thought believes that scientific concepts have no inward history, i.e., do not undergo development but are absorbed ready-made through a process of understanding and assimilation. Most educational theories and methods are still based on this view. It is nevertheless a view that fails to stand up under scrutiny, either theoretically or in its practical applications. As we know from investigations of the process of concept formation, a concept is more than the sum of certain associative bonds formed by memory, more than a mere mental habit; it is a complex and genuine act of thought that cannot be taught by drilling but can be accomplished only when the child's mental development itself has reached the requisite

82

level. At any age, a concept embodied in a word represents an act of generalization. But word meanings evolve. When a new word has been learned by the child, its development is barely starting; the word at first is a generalization of the most primitive type; as the child's intellect develops, it is replaced by generalizations of a higher and higher type — a process that leads in the end to the formation of true concepts. The development of concepts, or word meanings, presupposes the development of many intellectual functions: deliberate attention, logical memory, abstraction, the ability to compare and to differentiate. These complex psychological processes cannot be mastered through the initial learning alone.

Practical experience also shows that direct teaching of concepts is impossible and fruitless. A teacher who tries to do this usually accomplishes nothing but empty verbalism, a parrotlike repetition of words by the child, simulating a knowledge of the corresponding concepts but actually covering up a vacuum.

Leo Tolstoy, with his profound understanding of the nature of word and meaning, realized more clearly than most other educators the impossibility of simply relaying a concept from teacher to pupil. He tells of his attempts to teach literary language to peasant children by first "translating" their own vocabulary into the language of folk tales, then translating the language of tales into literary Russian. He found that one could not teach children literary language by artificial explanations, compulsive memorizing, and repetition, as one teaches a foreign language. Tolstoy writes:

> We have to admit that we attempted several times . . . to do this, and always met with an invincible distaste on the part of the children, which shows that we were on the wrong track. These experiments have left me with the certainty that it is quite impossible to explain the meaning of a word. . . . When you explain any word, the word "impression," for instance, you put in its place another equally incomprehensible word, or a whole series of words, with the connection between them as incomprehensible as the word itself.

What the child needs, says Tolstoy, is a chance to acquire new concepts and words from the general linguistic context.

When he has heard or read an unknown word in an otherwise comprehensible sentence, and another time in another sentence, he begins to have a hazy idea of the new concept; sooner or later he will . . . feel the need to use that word — and once he has used it, the word and the concept are his. . . . But to give the pupil new concepts deliberately . . . is, I am convinced, as impossible and futile as teaching a child to walk by the laws of equilibrium [*43*, p. 143].

The second conception of the evolution of scientific concepts does not deny the existence of a developmental process in the schoolchild's mind; it holds, however, that this process does not differ in any essential from the development of the concepts formed by the child in his everyday experience and that it is pointless to consider the two processes separately. What is the basis for this view?

The literature in this field shows that in studying concept formation in childhood most investigators have used everyday concepts formed by children without systematic instruction. The laws based on these data are assumed to apply also to the child's scientific concepts, and no checking of this assumption is deemed necessary. Only a few of the more perspicacious modern students of child thought question the legitimacy of such an extension. Piaget draws a sharp line between the child's ideas of reality developed mainly through his own mental efforts and those that were decisively influenced by adults; he designates the first group as *spontaneous*, the second as *nonspontaneous*, and admits that the latter may deserve independent investigation. In this respect, he goes farther and deeper than any of the other students of children's concepts.

At the same time, there are errors in Piaget's reasoning that detract from the value of his views. Although he holds that the child in forming a concept stamps it with the characteristics of his own mentality, Piaget tends to apply this thesis only to spontaneous concepts and assumes that they alone can truly enlighten us on the special qualities of child thought; he fails to see the interaction between the two kinds of concepts and the bonds that unite them into a total system of concepts in the course of the child's intellectual development. These errors lead to yet another. It is one of the basic tenets of Piaget's theory that progressive socialization of thinking is the very essence of the child's mental development. But if his views on the nature of nonspontaneous concepts were correct, it would follow that such an important factor in the socialization of thought as school learning is unrelated to the inner developmental processes. This inconsistency is the weak spot of Piaget's theory, both theoretically and practically.

Theoretically, socialization of thought is seen by Piaget as a mechanical abolition of the characteristics of the child's own thought, their gradual withering away. All that is new in development comes from without, replacing the child's own modes of thought. Throughout childhood, there is a ceaseless conflict between the two mutually antagonistic forms of thinking, with a series of compromises at each successive developmental level, until adult thought wins out. The child's own nature plays no constructive part in his intellectual progress. When Piaget says that nothing is more important for effective teaching than a thorough knowledge of spontaneous child thought [33], he is apparently prompted by the idea that child thought must be known as any enemy must be known in order to be fought successfully.

We shall counter these erroneous premises with the premise that the development of nonspontaneous concepts must possess all the traits peculiar to child thought at each developmental level because these concepts are not simply acquired by rote but evolve with the aid of strenuous mental activity on the part of the child himself. We believe that the two processes — the development of spontaneous and of nonspontaneous concepts — are related and constantly influence each other. They are parts of a single process: the development of concept formation, which is affected by varying external and internal conditions but is essentially a unitary process, not a conflict of antagonistic, mutually exclusive forms of mentation. Instruction is one of the principal sources of the schoolchild's concepts and is also a powerful force in directing their evolution; it determines the fate of his total mental development. If so, the results of the psychological study of children's concepts can be applied to the problems of teaching in a manner very different from that envisioned by Piaget.

Before discussing these premises in detail, we want to set forth our own reasons for differentiating between spontaneous and nonspontaneous — in particular scientific — concepts and for subjecting the latter to special study.

First, we know from simple observation that concepts form and develop under entirely different inner and outer conditions, depending on whether they originate in classroom instruction or in the child's personal experience. Even the motives prompting the child to form the two kinds of concepts are not the same. The mind faces different problems when assimilating concepts at school and when left to its own devices. When we impart systematic knowledge to the child, we teach him many things that he cannot directly see or experience. Since scientific and spontaneous concepts differ in their relation to the child's experience, and in the child's attitude toward their objects, they may be expected to follow differing developmental paths from their inception to their final form.

The singling-out of scientific concepts as an object of study also has a heuristic value. At present, psychology has only two ways of studying concept formation. One deals with the child's real concepts but uses methods — such as verbal definition — that do not penetrate below the surface; the other permits incomparably deeper psychological analysis, but only through studying the formation of artificially devised experimental concepts. An urgent methodological problem confronting us is to find ways of studying *real* concepts in *depth* — to find a method that could utilize the results already obtained by the two methods used so far. The most promising approach to the problem would seem to be the study of scientific concepts, which are real concepts yet are formed under our eyes almost in the fashion of artificial concepts.

Finally, the study of scientific concepts as such has important implications for education and instruction. Even though these concepts are not absorbed ready-made, instruction and learning play a leading role in their acquisition. To uncover the complex relationship between instruction and the development of scientific concepts is an important practical task.

These were the considerations that guided us in separating scientific from everyday concepts and subjecting them to comparative study. To illustrate the kind of question we tried to answer, let us take the concept "brother" — a typical everyday concept, which Piaget used so skillfully to establish a whole series of peculiarities of child thought — and compare it with the concept "exploitation," to which the child is introduced in his social science classes. Is their development the same, or is it different? Does "exploitation" merely repeat the developmental course of "brother," or is it, psychologically, a concept of a different type? We submit that the two concepts must differ in their development as well as in their functioning and that these two variants of the process of concept formation must influence each other's evolution.

II

To study the relationship between the development of scientific and that of everyday concepts, we need a yardstick for comparing them. To construct a measuring device, we must know the typical characteristics of everyday concepts at school age and the direction of their development during that period.

Piaget demonstrated that the schoolchild's concepts are marked primarily by his lack of conscious awareness of relationships, though he handles relationships correctly in a spontaneous, unreflective way. Piaget asked seven- to eight-year-olds the meaning of the word *because* in the sentence, "I won't go to school tomorrow because I am sick." Most of the children answered, "It means that he is sick"; others said, "It means that he won't go to school." A child is unable to realize that the question does not refer to the separate facts of sickness and of school absence but to their connection. Yet he certainly grasps the meaning of the sentence. Spontaneously, he uses *because* correctly, but he does not know how to use it deliberately. Thus, he cannot supply a correct ending to the sentence, "The man fell off his bicycle because. . . ." Often he will substitute a consequence ("because he broke his arm") for the cause. Child thought is nondeliberate and unconscious of itself. How, then, does the child eventually reach awareness and mastery of his own thoughts? To explain the process, Piaget cites two psychological laws.

One is the law of awareness, formulated by Claparède, who proved by very interesting experiments that awareness of difference precedes awareness of likeness. The child quite naturally responds in similar ways to objects that are alike and has no need to become aware of his mode of response, while dissimilarity creates a state of maladaptation which leads to awareness. Claparède's law states that the more smoothly we use a relationship in action, the less conscious we are of it; we become aware of what we are doing in proportion to the difficulty we experience in adapting to a situation.

Piaget uses Claparède's law to explain the development of thinking that takes place between the seventh and the twelfth year. During that period the child's mental operations repeatedly come in conflict with adult thinking. He suffers failures and defeats because of the deficiencies of his logic, and these painful experiences create the need to become aware of his concepts.

Realizing that need is not a sufficient explanation for any developmental change, Piaget supplements Claparède's law by the law of shift, or displacement. To become conscious of a mental operation means to transfer it from the plane of action to that of language, i.e., to re-create it in the imagination so that it can be expressed in words. This change is neither quick nor smooth. The law states that mastering an operation on the higher plane of verbal thought presents the same difficulties as the earlier mastering of that operation on the plane of action. This accounts for the slow progress.

These interpretations do not appear adequate. Claparède's findings may have a different explanation. Our own experimental studies suggest that the child becomes aware of differences earlier than of likenesses, not because differences lead to malfunctioning, but because awareness of similarity requires a more advanced structure of generalization and conceptualization than awareness of dissimilarity. In analyzing the development of concepts of difference and likeness, we found that consciousness of likeness presupposes the formation of a generalization, or of a concept, embracing the objects that are alike; consciousness of difference requires no such generalization — it may come about in other ways. The fact that the developmental sequence of these two concepts reverses the sequence of the earlier behavioral handling of similarity and difference is not unique. Our experiments established, for instance, that the child responds to pictorially represented action earlier than to the representation of an object, but becomes fully conscious of the object earlier than of action.*

The law of shift is an example of the widespread genetic theory according to which certain events or patterns observed in the early stages of a developmental process will recur in its advanced stages. The traits that do recur often blind the observer to significant differences caused by the fact that the later processes take place on a higher developmental level. We can dispense with discussing the principle of repetition as such, since we are concerned merely with its explanatory value in respect to the growth of awareness. The law of shift, like the law of awareness, may at best answer the question of why the schoolchild is not conscious of his concepts; it cannot explain how consciousness is achieved. We must look for another hypothesis to account for that decisive event in the child's mental development.

According to Piaget, the schoolchild's lack of awareness is a residue of his waning egocentrism, which still retains its influence in the sphere of verbal thought just beginning to form at that time. Consciousness is achieved when mature socialized thinking crowds out the residual egocentrism from the level of verbal thought.

Such an explanation of the nature of the schoolchild's con-

* Identical pictures were shown two groups of preschool children of similar age and developmental level. One group was asked to act out the picture — which would indicate the degree of their immediate grasp of its content; the other group was asked to tell about it in words, a task requiring a measure of conceptually mediated understanding. It was found that the "actors" rendered the sense of the represented action situation, while the narrators enumerated separate objects.

cepts, based essentially on his general inability to become fully conscious of his acts, does not stand up in the face of facts. Various studies have shown that it is precisely during early school age that the higher intellectual functions, whose main features are reflective awareness and deliberate control, come to the fore in the developmental process. Attention, previously involuntary, becomes voluntary and increasingly dependent on the child's own thinking; mechanical memory changes to logical memory guided by meaning, and can now be deliberately used by the child. One might say that both attention and memory become "logical" and voluntary, since control of a function is the counterpart of one's consciousness of it. Nevertheless, the fact established by Piaget cannot be denied: The schoolchild, though growing steadily in awareness and mastery, is not aware of his conceptual operations. All the basic mental functions become conscious and deliberate during school age, *except* intellect itself.

To resolve this seeming paradox, we must turn to the basic laws governing psychological development. One of them is that consciousness and control appear only at a late stage in the development of a function, after it has been used and practiced unconsciously and spontaneously. In order to subject a function to intellectual and volitional control, we must first possess it.

The stage of undifferentiated functions in infancy is followed by the differentiation and development of perception in early childhood and the development of memory in the preschooler, to mention only the outstanding aspects of mental development at each age. Attention, which is a correlate of the structuring of what is perceived and remembered, participates in this development. Consequently, the child about to enter school possesses, in a fairly mature form, the functions he must next learn to subject to conscious control. But concepts — or rather preconcepts, as they should be called at that stage — are barely beginning to evolve from complexes at that time, and it would indeed be a miracle if the child were able to become conscious of them and to govern them, during the same period. For this to be possible, consciousness would not merely have to take possession of its single functions but to create them.

Before continuing, we want to clarify the term *consciousness* as we use it in speaking of nonconscious functions "becoming conscious." (We use the term *nonconscious* to distinguish what is not yet conscious from the Freudian "unconscious" resulting from repression, which is a late development, an effect of a relatively high differentiation of consciousness.) The activity of consciousness can take different directions; it may illumine only a few aspects of a thought or an act. I have just tied a knot — I have done so consciously, yet I cannot explain how I did it, because my awareness was centered on the knot rather than on my own motions, the *how* of my action. When the latter becomes the object of my awareness, I shall have become fully conscious. We use *consciousness* to denote awareness of the activity of the mind — the consciousness of being conscious. A preschool child who, in response to the question, "Do you know your name?" tells his name lacks this self-reflective awareness: He knows his name but is not conscious of knowing it.

Piaget's studies showed that introspection begins to develop only during the school years. This process has a good deal in common with the development of external perception and observation in the transition from infancy to early childhood, when the child passes from primitive wordless perception to perception of objects guided by and expressed in words — perception in terms of meaning. Similarly, the schoolchild passes from unformulated to verbalized introspection; he perceives his own psychic processes as meaningful. But perception in terms of meaning always implies a degree of generalization. Consequently, the transition to verbalized self-observation denotes a beginning process of generalization of the inner forms of activity. The shift to a new type of inner perception means also a shift to a higher type of inner activity, since a new way of seeing things opens up new possibilities for handling them. A chessplayer's moves are determined by what he sees on the board; when his perception of the game changes, his strategy will also change. In perceiving some of our own acts in a generalizing fashion, we isolate them from our total mental activity and are thus enabled to focus on this process as such and to enter into a new relationship to it. In this way, becoming conscious of our operations and viewing each as a process of a certain *kind* — such as remembering or imagining — leads to their mastery.

School instruction induces the generalizing kind of perception and thus plays a decisive role in making the child conscious of his own mental processes. Scientific concepts, with their hierarchical system of interrelationships, seem to be the medium within which awareness and mastery first develop, to be transferred later to other concepts and other areas of thought. Reflective consciousness comes to the child through the portals of scientific concepts.

Piaget's characterization of the child's spontaneous concepts as nonconscious and nonsystematic tends to confirm our thesis. The implication that *spontaneous,* when applied to concepts, is a synonym of *nonconscious* is obvious throughout his writings, and the basis for this is easily seen. In operating with spontaneous concepts, the child is not conscious of them because his attention is always centered on the object to which the concept refers, never on the act of thought itself. Piaget's view that spontaneous concepts exist for the child outside any systematic context is equally clear. According to him, if we wish to discover and explore the child's own spontaneous idea hidden behind the nonspontaneous concept he voices, we must begin by freeing it from all ties to a system. This approach resulted in the kind of answers expressing the child's nonmediated attitude toward objects that fill all the books of Piaget.

To us it seems obvious that a concept can become subject to consciousness and deliberate control only when it is a part of a system. If consciousness means generalization, generalization in turn means the formation of a superordinate concept that includes the given concept as a particular case. A superordinate concept implies the existence of a series of subordinate concepts, and it also presupposes a hierarchy of concepts of different levels of generality. Thus the given concept is placed within a system of relationships of generality. The following example may illustrate the function of varying degrees of generality in the emergence of a system: A child learns the word *flower,* and shortly afterwards the word *rose;* for a long time the concept "flower," though more widely applicable than "rose," cannot be said to be more general for the child. It does not include and subordinate "rose" — the two are interchangeable and juxtaposed. When "flower" becomes generalized, the relationship of "flower" and "rose," as well as of "flower" and other subordinate concepts, also changes in the child's mind. A system is taking shape.

In the scientific concepts that the child acquires in school, the relationship to an object is mediated from the start by some other concept. Thus the very notion of scientific concept implies a certain position in relation to other concepts, i.e., a place within a system of concepts. It is our contention that the rudiments of systematization first enter the child's mind by way of his contact with scientific concepts and are then transferred to everyday concepts, changing their psychological structure from the top down.

III

The interrelation of scientific and spontaneous concepts is a special case within a much broader subject: the relation of school instruction to the mental development of the child. Several theories concerning this relationship have been advanced in the past, and the question remains one of the major preoccupations of Soviet psychology. We shall review three attempts to answer it, in order to place our own study within the broader context.

The first and still most widely held theory considers instruction and development to be mutually independent. Development is seen as a process of maturation subject to natural laws, and instruction as the utilization of the opportunities created by development. Typical of this school of thought are its attempts to separate with great care the products of development from those of instruction, supposedly to find them in their pure form. No investigator has yet been able to achieve this. The blame is usually laid on inadequate methods, and the failures are compensated for by redoubled speculative analyses. These efforts to divide the child's intellectual equipment into two categories may go hand in hand with the notion that development can run its normal course and reach a high level without any assistance from instruction — that even children who never attend school can develop the highest forms of thinking accessible to human beings. More often, however, this theory is modified to take into account a relationship that obviously exists between development and instruction: The former creates the potentialities; the latter realizes them. Education is seen as a kind of superstructure erected over maturation; or, to change the metaphor, education is related to development as consumption to production. A one-sided relationship is thus conceded: Learning depends on development, but the course of development is not affected by learning.

This theory rests on the simple observation that any instruction demands a certain degree of maturity of certain functions: One cannot teach a one-year-old to read, or a three-year-old to write. The analysis of learning is thus reduced to determining the developmental level that various functions must reach for instruction to become feasible. When the child's memory has progressed enough to enable him to memorize the alphabet, when his attention can be held by a boring task, when his thinking has matured to the point where he can grasp the connection between sign and sound — then instruction in writing may begin. According to this variant of the first theory, instruction hobbles behind development. Development must complete certain cycles before instruction can begin.

The truth of this last statement is obvious; a necessary minimum level does exist. Nevertheless, this one-sided view results in a series of misconceptions. Suppose the child's memory, attention, and thinking have developed to the point where he can be taught writing and arithmetic; does the study of writing and arithmetic do anything to his memory, attention, and thinking, or does it not? Traditional psychology answers: Yes, in so far as they exercise these functions; but the process of development as such does not change; nothing new happens in the mental growth of the child; he has learned to write — that is all. This view, characteristic of old-fashioned educational theory, also colors the writings of Piaget, who believes that the child's thinking goes through certain phases and stages regardless of any instruction he may receive; instruction remains an extraneous factor. The gauge of the child's level of development is not what he has learned through instruction but the manner in which he thinks on subjects about which he has been taught nothing. Here the separation — indeed, the opposition — of instruction and development is carried to its extreme.

The second theory concerning development and instruction identifies the two processes. Originally expounded by James, it bases both processes on association and habit formation, thus rendering instruction synonymous with development. This view enjoys a certain revival at present, with Thorndike as its chief protagonist. Reflexology, which has translated associationism into the language of physiology, sees the intellectual development of the child as a gradual accumulation of conditioned reflexes; and learning is viewed in exactly the same way. Since instruction and development are identical, no question of any concrete relationship between them can arise.

The third school of thought, represented by Gestalt psychology, tries to reconcile the two foregoing theories while avoiding their pitfalls. Although this eclecticism results in a somewhat inconsistent approach, a certain synthesis of the two opposite views is achieved. Koffka states that all development has two aspects, maturation and learning. Although this means accepting in a less extreme form both of the older points of view, the new theory represents an improvement on the two others, in three ways.

First, Koffka admits some interdependence between the two aspects of development. On the basis of a number of facts, he demonstrates that maturation of an organ is contingent on its functioning, which improves through learning and practice. Maturation, in turn, provides new opportunities for learning. But Koffka merely postulates mutual influence without examining its nature in detail. Second, this theory introduces a new conception of the educational process itself as the formation of new structures and the perfecting of old ones. Instruction is thus accorded a meaningful structural role. A basic characteristic of any structure is its independence from its original substance — it can be transferred to other media. Once a child has formed a certain structure, or learned a certain operation, he will be able to apply it in other areas. We have given him a pennyworth of instruction, and he has gained a small fortune in development. The third point in which this theory compares favorably with the older ones is its view of the temporal relation between instruction and development. Since instruction given in one area can transform and reorganize other areas of child thought, it may not only follow maturing or keep in step with it but also precede it and further its progress. The admission that different temporal sequences are equally possible and important is a contribution by the eclectic theory that should not be underestimated.

This theory brings us face to face with an old issue reappearing in a new guise: the almost forgotten theory of formal discipline, usually associated with Herbart. It maintained that instruction in certain subjects develops the mental faculties in general, besides imparting the knowledge of the subject and specific skills. In practice, this led to the most reactionary forms of schooling, such as the Russian and the German "classical gymnasiums," which inordinately stressed Greek and Latin as sources of "formal discipline." The system was eventually discarded because it did not meet the practical aims of modern bourgeois education. Within psychology itself, Thorndike, in a series of investigations, did his best to discredit formal discipline as a myth and to prove that instruction had no far-reaching effects on development. His criticism is convincing in so far as it applies to the ludicrous exaggerations of the doctrine of formal discipline, but it does not touch its valuable kernel.

In his effort to disprove Herbart's conception, Thorndike experimented with the narrowest, most specialized, and most elementary functions. From the point of view of a theory that reduces all learning to the formation of associative bonds, the choice of activity would make little difference. In some experiments he gave his subjects practice in distinguishing between the relative lengths of lines and then tried to establish whether this practice increased their ability to distinguish between sizes of angles. Naturally, he found that it did not. The influence of instruction on development had been postulated by the theory of formal discipline only in relation to such subjects as mathematics or languages, which involve vast complexes of psychic functions. The ability to gauge the length of lines may not affect the ability to distinguish between angles, but the study of the native language — with its attendant sharpening of concepts — may still have some bearing on the study of arithmetic. Thorndike's work merely makes it appear likely that there are two kinds of instruction: the narrowly specialized training in some skill, such as typing, involving habit formation and exercise and more often found in trade schools for adults, and the kind of instruction given schoolchildren, which activates large areas of consciousness. The idea of formal discipline may have little to do with the first kind but may well prove to be valid for the second. It stands to reason that in the higher processes emerging during the cultural development of the child, formal discipline must play a role that it does not play in the more elementary processes: All the higher functions have in common awareness, abstraction, and control. In line with Thorndike's theoretical conceptions, the qualitative differences between the lower and the higher functions are ignored in his studies of the transfer of training.

In formulating our own tentative theory of the relationship between instruction and development, we take our departure from four series of investigations [2]. Their common purpose was to uncover these complex interrelations in certain definite areas of school instruction: reading and writing, grammar, arithmetic, natural science, and social science. The specific inquiries concerned such topics as the mastering of the decimal system in relation to the development of the concept of number; the child's awareness of his operations in solving mathematical problems; the processes of constructing and solving problems by first-graders. Much interesting material came to light on the development of oral and written language during school age, the consecutive levels of understanding of figurative meaning, the influence of mastering grammatical structures on the course of mental development, the understanding of relationships in the study of social science and natural science. The investigations focused on the level of maturity of psychic functions at the beginning of schooling, and the influence of schooling on their development; on the temporal sequence of instruction and development; on the "formal discipline" function of the various subjects of instruction. We shall discuss these issues in succession.

1. In our first series of studies, we examined the level of development of the psychic functions requisite for learning the basic school subjects — reading and writing, arithmetic, natural science. We found that at the beginning of instruction these functions could not be considered mature, even in the children who proved able to master the curriculum very successfully. Written language is a good illustration. Why does writing come so hard to the schoolchild that at certain periods there is a lag of as much as six or eight years between his "linguistic age" in speaking and in writing? This used to be explained by the novelty of writing: As a new function, it must repeat the developmental stages of speech; therefore the writing of an eight-year-old must resemble the speech of a two-year-old. This explanation is patently insufficient. A two-year-old uses few words and a simple syntax because his vocabulary is small and his knowledge of more complex sentence structures nonexistent; but the schoolchild possesses the vocabulary and the grammatical forms for writing, since they are the same as for oral speech. Nor can the difficulties of mastering the mechanics of writing account for the tremendous lag between the schoolchild's oral and written language.

Our investigation has shown that the development of writing does not repeat the developmental history of speaking. Written speech is a separate linguistic function, differing from oral speech in both structure and mode of functioning. Even its minimal development requires a high level of abstraction. It is speech in thought and image only, lacking the musical, expressive, intonational qualities of oral speech. In learning to write, the child must disengage himself from the sensory aspect of speech and replace words by images of words. Speech that is merely imagined and that requires symbolization of the

sound image in written signs (i.e., a second degree of symbolization) naturally must be as much harder than oral speech for the
child as algebra is harder than arithmetic. Our studies show
that it is the abstract quality of written language that is the
main stumbling block, not the underdevelopment of small
muscles or any other mechanical obstacles.

Writing is also speech without an interlocutor, addressed to
an absent or an imaginary person or to no one in particular —
a situation new and strange to the child. Our studies show that
he has little motivation to learn writing when we begin to
teach it. He feels no need for it and has only a vague idea of
its usefulness. In conversation, every sentence is prompted by a
motive. Desire or need lead to request, question to answer,
bewilderment to explanation. The changing motives of the
interlocutors determine at every moment the turn oral speech
will take. It does not have to be consciously directed — the
dynamic situation takes care of that. The motives for writing
are more abstract, more intellectualized, further removed from
immediate needs. In written speech, we are obliged to create the
situation, to represent it to ourselves. This demands detachment
from the actual situation.

Writing also requires deliberate analytical action on the part
of the child. In speaking, he is hardly conscious of the sounds he
pronounces and quite unconscious of the mental operations he
performs. In writing, he must take cognizance of the sound
structure of each word, dissect it, and reproduce it in alphabeti-
cal symbols, which he must have studied and memorized before.
In the same deliberate way, he must put words in a certain
sequence to form a sentence. Written language demands conscious work because its relationship to inner speech is different
from that of oral speech: The latter precedes inner speech in
the course of development, while written speech follows inner
speech and presupposes its existence (the act of writing imply-
ing a translation from inner speech). But the grammar of
thought is not the same in the two cases. One might even say
that the syntax of inner speech is the exact opposite of the
syntax of written speech, with oral speech standing in the
middle.

Inner speech is condensed, abbreviated speech. Written speech is deployed to its fullest extent, more complete than oral speech. Inner speech is almost entirely predicative because the situation, the subject of thought, is always known to the thinker. Written speech, on the contrary, must explain the situation fully in order to be intelligible. The change from maximally compact inner speech to maximally detailed written speech requires what might be called deliberate semantics — deliberate structuring of the web of meaning.

All these traits of written speech explain why its development in the schoolchild falls far behind that of oral speech. The discrepancy is caused by the child's proficiency in spontaneous, unconscious activity and his lack of skill in abstract, deliberate activity. As our studies showed, the psychological functions on which written speech is based have not even begun to develop in the proper sense when instruction in writing starts. It must build on barely emerging, rudimentary processes.

Similar results were obtained in the fields of arithmetic, grammar, and natural science. In every case, the requisite functions are immature when instruction begins. We shall briefly discuss the case of grammar, which presents some special features.

Grammar is a subject which seems to be of little practical use. Unlike other school subjects, it does not give the child new skills. He conjugates and declines before he enters school. The opinion has even been voiced that school instruction in grammar could be dispensed with. We can only reply that our analysis clearly showed the study of grammar to be of paramount importance for the mental development of the child.

The child does have a command of the grammar of his native tongue long before he enters school, but it is unconscious, acquired in a purely structural way, like the phonetic composition of words. If you ask a young child to produce a combination of sounds, for example *sk,* you will find that its deliberate articulation is too hard for him; yet within a structure, as in the word *Moscow,* he pronounces the same sounds with ease. The same is true of grammar. The child will use the correct case or tense within a sentence but cannot decline or conjugate a word on request. He may not acquire new grammatical or syntactic forms in school but, thanks to instruction in grammar and writing, he does become aware of what he is doing and learns to use his skills consciously. Just as the child realizes for the first time in learning to write that the word *Moscow* consists of the sounds *m-o-s-k-ow* and learns to pronounce each one separately, he also learns to construct sentences, to do consciously what he has been doing unconsciously in speaking. Grammar and writing help the child to rise to a higher level of speech development.

Thus our investigation shows that the development of the psychological foundations for instruction in basic subjects does not precede instruction but unfolds in a continuous interaction with the contributions of instruction.

2. Our second series of investigations centered on the temporal relation between the processes of instruction and the development of the corresponding psychological functions. We found that instruction usually precedes development. The child acquires certain habits and skills in a given area before he learns to apply them consciously and deliberately. There is never complete parallelism between the course of instruction and the development of the corresponding functions.

Instruction has its own sequences and organization, it follows a curriculum and a timetable, and its rules cannot be expected to coincide with the inner laws of the developmental processes it calls to life. On the basis of our studies, we tried to plot curves of the progress of instruction and of the participating psychological functions; far from coinciding, these curves showed an exceedingly complex relationship.

For example, the different steps in learning arithmetic may be of unequal value for mental development. It often happens that three or four steps in instruction add little to the child's understanding of arithmetic, and then, with the fifth step, something clicks; the child has grasped a general principle, and his developmental curve rises markedly. For this particular child, the fifth operation was decisive, but this cannot be a general rule. The turning points at which a general principle becomes clear to the child cannot be set in advance by the curriculum. The child is not taught the decimal system as such; he is taught to write figures, to add and to multiply, to solve problems, and out of all this some general concept of the decimal system eventually emerges.

When the child learns some arithmetical operation or some scientific concept, the development of that operation or concept has only begun. Our study shows that the curve of development does not coincide with the curve of school instruction; by and large, instruction precedes development.

3. Our third series of investigations resembles Thorndike's studies of the transfer of training, except that we experimented with subjects of school instruction and with the higher rather than the elementary functions, i.e., with subjects and functions which could be expected to be meaningfully related.

We found that intellectual development, far from following Thorndike's atomistic model, is not compartmentalized according to topics of instruction. Its course is much more unitary, and the different school subjects interact in contributing to it. While the processes of instruction follow their own logical order, they awaken and direct a system of processes in the child's mind which is hidden from direct observation and subject to its own developmental laws. To uncover these developmental processes stimulated by instruction is one of the basic tasks of the psychological study of learning.

Specifically, our experiments brought out the following interrelated facts: The psychological prerequisites for instruction in different school subjects are to a large extent the same; instruction in a given subject influences the development of the higher functions far beyond the confines of that particular subject; the main psychic functions involved in studying various subjects are interdependent — their common bases are consciousness and deliberate mastery, the principal contributions of the school years. It follows from these findings that all the basic school subjects act as formal discipline, each facilitating the learning of the others; the psychological functions stimulated by them develop in one complex process.

4. In the fourth series of studies, we attacked a problem which has not received sufficient attention in the past but which we consider of focal importance for the study of learning and development.

Most of the psychological investigations concerned with school learning measured the level of mental development of the child by making him solve certain standardized problems. The problems he was able to solve by himself were supposed to indicate the level of his mental development at the particular time. But in this way only the completed part of the child's development can be measured, which is far from the whole story. We tried a different approach. Having found that the mental age of two children was, let us say, eight, we gave each of them harder problems than he could manage on his own and provided some slight assistance: the first step in a solution, a leading question, or some other form of help. We discovered that one child could, in co-operation, solve problems designed for twelve-year-olds, while the other could not go beyond problems intended for nine-year-olds. The discrepancy between a child's actual mental age and the level he reaches in solving problems with assistance indicates the zone of his proximal development; in our example, this zone is four for the first child and one for the second. Can we truly say that their mental development is the same? Experience has shown that the child with the larger zone of proximal development will do much better in school. This measure gives a more helpful clue than mental age does to the dynamics of intellectual progress.

Psychologists today cannot share the layman's belief that imitation is a mechanical activity and that anyone can imitate almost anything if shown how. To imitate, it is necessary to possess the means of stepping from something one knows to something new. With assistance, every child can do more than he can by himself — though only within the limits set by the state of his development. Koehler found that a chimpanzee can imitate only those intelligent acts of other apes that he could have performed on his own. Persistent training, it is true, can induce him to perform much more complicated actions, but these are carried out mechanically and have all the earmarks of meaningless habits rather than of insightful solutions. The cleverest animal is incapable of intellectual development through imitation. It can be drilled to perform specific acts, but the new habits do not result in new general abilities. In this sense, it can be said that animals are unteachable.

In the child's development, on the contrary, imitation and instruction play a major role. They bring out the specifically human qualities of the mind and lead the child to new developmental levels. In learning to speak, as in learning school subjects, imitation is indispensable. What the child can do in cooperation today he can do alone tomorrow. Therefore the only good kind of instruction is that which marches ahead of development and leads it; it must be aimed not so much at the ripe as at the ripening functions. It remains necessary to determine the lowest threshold at which instruction in, say, arithmetic may begin since a certain minimal ripeness of functions is required. But we must consider the upper threshold as well; instruction must be oriented toward the future, not the past.

For a time, our schools favored the "complex" system of instruction, which was believed to be adapted to the child's ways of thinking. In offering the child problems he was able to handle without help, this method failed to utilize the zone of proximal development and to lead the child to what he could not yet do. Instruction was oriented to the child's weakness rather than his strength, thus encouraging him to remain at the preschool stage of development.

For each subject of instruction there is a period when its influence is most fruitful because the child is most receptive to it. It has been called the *sensitive period* by Montessori and other educators. The term is used also in biology, for the periods in ontogenetic development when the organism is particularly responsive to influences of certain kinds. During that period an influence that has little effect earlier or later may radically affect the course of development. But the existence of an optimum time for instruction in a given subject cannot be explained in purely biological terms, at least not for such complex processes as written speech. Our investigation demonstrated the social and cultural nature of the development of the higher

functions during these periods, i.e., its dependence on co-operation with adults and on instruction. Montessori's data, however,
retain their significance. She found, for instance, that if a child
is taught to write early, at four and a half or five years of age,
he responds by "explosive writing," an abundant and imaginative use of written speech that is never duplicated by children
a few years older. This is a striking example of the strong influence that instruction can have when the corresponding functions have not yet fully matured. The existence of sensitive
periods for all subjects of instruction is fully supported by the
data of our studies. The school years as a whole are the optimum period for instruction in operations that require awareness and deliberate control; instruction in these operations
maximally furthers the development of the higher psychological
functions while they are maturing. This applies also to the
development of the scientific concepts to which school instruction introduces the child.

IV

Zh. I. Shif, under our guidance, conducted an investigation
of the development of scientific and everyday concepts during
school age [*37*]. Its chief purpose was to test experimentally our
working hypothesis of the development of scientific concepts
compared with everyday concepts. The child was given structurally similar problems dealing with either scientific or "ordinary" material, and his solutions were compared. The experiments included making up stories from series of pictures that
showed the beginning of an action, its continuation, and its end,
and completing fragments of sentences ending in *because* or *although;* these tests were complemented by clinical discussion.
The material for one series of tests was taken from social science
courses of the second and fourth grades. The second series used
simple situations of everyday life, such as: "The boy went to
the movies because . . . ," "The girl cannot yet read, although
. . . ," "He fell off his bicycle because. . . ." Supplementary
methods of study included testing the extent of the child's
knowledge and observation during lessons specially organized

for the purpose. The children we studied were primary school pupils.

Analysis of the data compared separately for each age group in the table below showed that as long as the curriculum supplies the necessary material *the development of scientific concepts runs ahead of the development of spontaneous concepts.*

CORRECT COMPLETIONS OF SENTENCE FRAGMENTS

	Second Grade	Fourth Grade*
	(per cent)	
Fragments ending in *because*		
Scientific concepts	79.7	81.8
Spontaneous concepts	59.0	81.3
Fragments ending in *although*		
Scientific concepts	21.3	79.5
Spontaneous concepts	16.2	65.5

How are we to explain the fact that problems involving scientific concepts are solved correctly more often than similar problems involving everyday concepts? We can at once dismiss the notion that the child is helped by factual information acquired at school and lacks experience in everyday matters. Our tests, like Piaget's, dealt entirely with things and relations familiar to the child and often spontaneously mentioned by him in conversation. No one would assume that a child knows less about bicycles, children, or school than about the class struggle, exploitation, or the Paris Commune. The advantage of familiarity is all on the side of the everyday concepts.

The child must find it hard to solve problems involving life situations because he lacks awareness of his concepts and therefore cannot operate with them at will as the task demands. A child of eight or nine uses *because* correctly in spontaneous conversation; he would never say that a boy fell and broke his leg *because* he was taken to the hospital. Yet that is the sort of thing he comes up with in experiments until the concept "be-

* In the Russian school system, children in the second and fourth grades would be, on the average, eight and ten years old. — *Editor*

cause" becomes fully conscious. On the other hand, he correctly finishes sentences on social science subjects: "Planned economy is possible in the U.S.S.R. because there is no private property — all land, factories, and plants belong to the workers and peasants." Why is he capable of performing the operation in this case? Because the teacher, working with the pupil, has explained, supplied information, questioned, corrected, and made the pupil explain. The child's concepts have been formed in the process of instruction, in collaboration with an adult. In finishing the sentence, he makes use of the fruits of that collaboration, this time independently. The adult's help, invisibly present, enables the child to solve such problems earlier than everyday problems.

At the same age level (second grade), *although* sentences present a different picture: Scientific concepts are not ahead of everyday ones. We know that adversative relations appear later than causal relations in the child's spontaneous thinking. A child of that age can learn to use *because* consciously because by then he has already mastered its spontaneous use. Not having mastered *although* in the same way, he naturally cannot use it deliberately in his "scientific" thinking; hence, the percentage of successes is equally low in both test series.

Our data show quick progress in the solution of problems involving everyday concepts: In the fourth grade *because* fragments are completed correctly with equal frequency for everyday and for scientific material. This bears out our assumption that mastering a higher level in the realm of scientific concepts also raises the level of spontaneous concepts. Once the child has achieved consciousness and control in one kind of concepts, all of the previously formed concepts are reconstructed accordingly.

The relationship between scientific and spontaneous concepts in the adversative category presents in the fourth grade a picture very similar to that of the causal category in the second grade. The percentage of correct solutions for tasks involving scientific concepts surpasses the percentage for those involving everyday concepts. If the dynamics are the same for both categories, everyday concepts may be expected to rise sharply in the next stage of development and finally to catch up with scientific concepts. Starting two years later, the whole process of the development of "although" would duplicate that of "because."

We believe that our data warrant the assumption that from the very beginning the child's scientific and his spontaneous concepts — for instance, "exploitation" and "brother" — *develop in reverse directions:* Starting far apart, they move to meet each other. This is the key point of our hypothesis.

The child becomes conscious of his spontaneous concepts relatively late; the ability to define them in words, to operate with them at will, appears long after he has acquired the concepts. He has the concept (i.e., knows the object to which the concept refers), but is not conscious of his own act of thought. The development of a scientific concept, on the other hand, usually *begins* with its verbal definition and its use in non-spontaneous operations — with working on the concept itself. It starts its life in the child's mind at the level that his spontaneous concepts reach only later.

A child's everyday concept, such as "brother," is saturated with experience. Yet, when he is asked to solve an abstract problem about a brother's brother, as in Piaget's experiments, he becomes confused. On the other hand, though he can correctly answer questions about "slavery," "exploitation," or "civil war," these concepts are schematic and lack the rich content derived from personal experience. They are filled in gradually, in the course of further schoolwork and reading. One might say that *the development of the child's spontaneous concepts proceeds upward, and the development of his scientific concepts downward,* to a more elementary and concrete level. This is a consequence of the different ways in which the two kinds of concepts emerge. The inception of a spontaneous concept can usually be traced to a face-to-face meeting with a concrete situation, while a scientific concept involves from the first a "mediated" attitude toward its object.

Though scientific and spontaneous concepts develop in reverse directions, the two processes are closely connected. The development of a spontaneous concept must have reached a certain level for the child to be able to absorb a related scientific concept. For example, historical concepts can begin to develop only when the child's everyday concept of the past is sufficiently differentiated — when his own life and the life of those around him can be fitted into the elementary generalization "in the past and now"; his geographic and sociological concepts must grow out of the simple schema "here and elsewhere." In working its slow way upward, an everyday concept clears a path for the scientific concept and its downward development. It creates a series of structures necessary for the evolution of a concept's more primitive, elementary aspects, which give it body and vitality. Scientific concepts in turn supply structures for the upward development of the child's spontaneous concepts toward consciousness and deliberate use. Scientific concepts grow down through spontaneous concepts; spontaneous concepts grow upward through scientific concepts.

The influence of scientific concepts on the mental development of the child is analogous to the effect of learning a foreign language, a process which is conscious and deliberate from the start. In one's native language, the primitive aspects of speech are acquired before the more complex ones. The latter presuppose some awareness of phonetic, grammatical, and syntactic forms. With a foreign language, the higher forms develop before spontaneous, fluent speech. The intellectualistic theories of language, such as Stern's, which place a full grasp of the relationship between sign and meaning at the very beginning of linguistic development, contain a measure of truth in the case of a foreign language. The child's strong points in a foreign language are his weak points in his native language, and vice versa. In his own language, the child conjugates and declines correctly, but without realizing it. He cannot tell the gender, the case, or the tense of the word he is using. In a foreign language, he distinguishes between masculine and feminine gender and is conscious of grammatical forms from the beginning.

Of phonetics, the same is true. Faultlessly articulating his native speech, the child is unconscious of the sounds he pronounces, and in learning to spell he has great difficulty in dividing a word into its constituent sounds. In a foreign language, he does this easily, and his writing does not lag behind his speech. It is the pronunciation, the "spontaneous phonetics," that he finds hard to master. Easy, spontaneous speech with a quick and sure command of grammatical structures comes to him only as the crowning achievement of long, arduous study.

Success in learning a foreign language is contingent on a certain degree of maturity in the native language. The child can transfer to the new language the system of meanings he already possesses in his own. The reverse is also true — a foreign language facilitates mastering the higher forms of the native language. The child learns to see his language as one particular system among many, to view its phenomena under more general categories, and this leads to awareness of his linguistic operations. Goethe said with truth that "he who knows no foreign language does not truly know his own."

It is not surprising that an analogy should exist between the interaction of the native and the foreign language and the interaction of scientific and spontaneous concepts, since both processes belong in the sphere of developing verbal thought. However, there are also essential differences between them. In foreign language study, attention centers on the exterior, sonal, physical aspects of verbal thought; in the development of scientific concepts, on its semantic aspect. The two developmental processes follow separate, though similar, paths.

Nevertheless, both suggest a single answer to the question of how new systems are formed that are structurally analogous to earlier ones: *written* speech, *foreign* language, *verbal* thought in general. The experimental evidence yielded by our studies disproves the theory of shift, or displacement, which states that the later stage repeats the course of the earlier one, including the recurrence of difficulties already overcome on the lower plane. All our evidence supports the hypothesis that analogous systems develop in reverse directions at the higher and at the lower levels, each system influencing the other and benefiting from the strong points of the other.

We can now turn to the interrelation of concepts in a system — the focal problem of our analysis.

Concepts do not lie in the child's mind like peas in a bag, without any bonds between them. If that were the case, no intellectual operation requiring co-ordination of thoughts would be possible, nor any general conception of the world. Not even separate concepts as such could exist; their very nature presupposes a system.

The study of the child's concepts at each age level shows that the degree of generality (plant, flower, rose) is the basic psychological variable according to which they can be meaningfully ordered. If every concept is a generalization, then the relationship between concepts is a relationship of generality. The logical aspect of that relationship has been studied much more fully than its genetic and psychological aspects. Our study attempts to fill this gap.

We compared the degree of generality of the child's real concepts with the phases and stages reached by the child in experimental concept formation: syncretism, complex, preconcept, and concept. Our aim was to find out whether a definite relationship existed between the structure of generalization typified by these phases and the degree of generality of concepts.

Concepts of differing degrees of generality may occur in one and the same generalizational structure. For instance, the ideas "flower" and "rose" may both be present at the stage of complex thinking. Correspondingly, concepts of equal generality may appear within different structures of generalization, e.g., "flower" may apply to any and all flowers at the complex stage as well as in conceptual thinking. We found, however, that in spite of this lack of complete correspondence each phase, or generalizational structure, has as its counterpart a specific level of generality, a specific relationship of superordinate and subordinate concepts, a typical combination of the concrete and the abstract. The term *flower*, it is true, may be equally general at the level of complex and of concept, but only in relation to the objects to which it refers. Equal generality here does not imply identity of all the psychological processes involved in the use of this term. Thus, in complex thinking the relationship of "flower" to "rose" is not superordination; the wider and the narrower concepts coexist on the same plane.

In our experiments a mute child learned without much difficulty the words *table, chair, bureau, couch, shelves,* and so on.

The term *furniture*, however, proved too hard to grasp. The same child, having successfully learned *shirt, hat, coat, pants,* etc., could not rise above the level of this series and master *clothes*. We found that at a certain level of development the child is incapable of moving "vertically" from one word meaning to another, i.e., of understanding their relationships of generality. All his concepts are on one level, refer directly to objects, and are delimited from one another in the same way that the objects themselves are delimited: Verbal thought is no more than a dependent component of perceptual, object-determined thought. Hence, this stage must be considered an early, presyncretic stage in the development of word meaning. The appearance of the first generalized concept, such as "furniture" or "clothes," is as significant a symptom of progress as the first meaningful word.

The higher levels in the development of word meanings are governed by the law of equivalence of concepts, according to which any concept can be formulated in terms of other concepts in a countless number of ways. We shall illustrate the schema underlying this law by an analogy not ideally accurate but close enough to serve the purpose.

If we imagine the totality of concepts as distributed over the surface of a globe, the location of every concept may be defined by means of a system of co-ordinates, corresponding to longitude and latitude in geography. One of these co-ordinates will indicate the location of a concept between the extremes of maximally generalized abstract conceptualization and the immediate sensory grasp of an object — i.e., its degree of concreteness and abstraction. The second co-ordinate will represent the objective reference of the concept, the locus within reality to which it applies. Two concepts applying to different areas of reality but comparable in degree of abstractness — e.g., plants and animals — could be conceived of as varying in latitude but having the same longitude. The geographical analogy breaks down in several details: The more generalized concept, for instance, applies to a broader area of content, which should be represented by a line, not a point. But it serves to convey the idea that to be adequately characterized each concept must be placed within two continua — one that represents objective content and another that represents acts of thought apprehending the content. Their intersection determines all the relationships of the given concept to others — its co-ordinate, superordinate, and subordinate concepts. This position of a concept within the total system of concepts may be called its measure of generality.

The manifold mutual relations of concepts on which the law of equivalence is based are determined by their respective measures of generality. Let us take two extreme examples: the child's early (presyncretic) words lacking any variation in degree of generality and the concepts of numbers developed through the study of arithmetic. In the first case, obviously, every concept can be expressed only through itself, never through other concepts. In the second case, any number may be expressed in countless ways, because of the infinity of numbers and because the concept of any number contains also all of its relationships to all other numbers. "One," for instance, may be expressed as "1000 minus 999" or, in general, as the difference between any two consecutive numbers, or as any number divided by itself, and in a myriad of other ways. This is a pure example of equivalence of concepts. In so far as equivalence depends on the relationships of generality between concepts, and these are specific for every generalizational structure, the latter determines the equivalence of concepts possible within its sphere.

The measure of generality determines not only the equivalence of concepts but also all of the intellectual operations possible with a given concept. All intellectual operations — comparisons, judgments, conclusions — require some movement within the net of co-ordinates we have outlined. Developmental changes in the structure of generalization cause changes also in these operations. For example, as higher levels of generality and equivalence of concepts are reached, it becomes easier for a child to remember thoughts independently of words. A young child must reproduce the exact words in which a meaning was conveyed to him. A schoolchild can already render a relatively complex meaning in his own words; thus his intellectual freedom increases. In pathological disturbances of conceptual thinking, the measure of generality of concepts is distorted, the balance between the abstract and the concrete is upset, and the relationship to other concepts becomes unstable. The mental act through which both the object and the object's relation to the concept are grasped loses its unity, and thought begins to run along broken, capricious, illogical lines.

One goal of our study of the child's real concepts was to find reliable indices of their structure of generalization. Only with their help could the genetic schema yielded by our experimental studies of artificial concepts be profitably applied to the child's developing real concepts. Such an index was finally discovered in the concept's measure of generality, which varies on the different levels of development, from syncretic formations to concepts proper. Analysis of the child's real concepts also helped us to determine how concepts differ at the various levels in their relationship to the object and to word meaning, and in the intellectual operations they make possible.

Furthermore, the investigation of real concepts complemented the experimental study by making it clear that every new stage in the development of generalization is built on generalizations of the preceding level; the products of the intellectual activity of the earlier phases are not lost. The inner bond between the consecutive phases could not be uncovered in our experiments because the subject had to discard, after each wrong solution, the generalizations he had formed, and start all over again. Also, the nature of the experimental objects did not permit their conceptualization in hierarchical terms.

The investigation of real concepts filled these gaps. The preschooler's ideas (which have the structure of complexes) were found to result, not from grouping images of individual objects, but from elaboration of generalizations predominant during an earlier phase. At a higher level, we found an analogous relationship between old and new formations in the development of arithmetical and algebraic concepts. The rise from preconcepts (which the schoolchild's arithmetical concepts usually are) to true concepts, such as the algebraic concepts of adolescents, is achieved by generalizing the generalizations of the earlier level. At the earlier stage certain aspects of objects had been abstracted and generalized into ideas of numbers. Algebraic concepts represent abstractions and generalizations of certain aspects of numbers, not objects, and thus signify a new departure — a new, higher plane of thought.

The new, higher concepts in turn transform the meaning of the lower. The adolescent who has mastered algebraic concepts has gained a vantage point from which he sees arithmetical concepts in a broader perspective. We saw this especially clearly in experimenting with shifts from the decimal to other numerical systems. As long as the child operates with the decimal system without having become conscious of it as such, he has not mastered the system but is, on the contrary, bound by it. When he becomes able to view it as a particular instance of the wider concept of a scale of notation, he can operate deliberately with this or any other numerical system. The ability to shift at will from one system to another (e.g., to "translate" from the decimal system into one that is based on five) is the criterion of this new level of consciousness, since it indicates the existence of a general concept of a system of numeration. In this as in other instances of passing from one level of meaning to the next, the child does not have to restructure separately all of his earlier concepts, which indeed would be a Sisyphean labor. Once a new structure has been incorporated into his thinking — usually through concepts recently acquired in school — it gradually spreads to the older concepts as they are drawn into the intellectual operations of the higher type.

Our investigation of children's real concepts throws a new light on another important issue in the theory of thought. The Wuerzburg school demonstrated that the course of directed thought is not governed by associative connections, but it did little to clarify the specific factors that actually determine this course. Gestalt psychology substituted the principle of structure for that of association but failed to distinguish thought proper from perception, memory, and all the other functions subject to structural laws; it repeated the pattern of the association theory in reducing all the functions to one level. Our investigations help to transcend this pattern by showing that thought of a higher level is governed by the relations of generality between concepts — a system of relations absent from perception and memory. Wertheimer has demonstrated that productive thinking is contingent on transferring the problem from the structure within which it was first apprehended to an entirely different context or structure. But to transfer an object of thought from structure A to structure B, one must transcend the given structural bonds, and this, as our studies show, requires shifting to a plane of greater generality, to a concept subsuming and governing both A and B.

We can now reaffirm on a sound basis of data that the *absence of a system* is the cardinal psychological difference distinguishing spontaneous from scientific concepts. It could be shown that all the peculiarities of child thought described by Piaget (such as syncretism, juxtaposition, insensitivity to contradiction) stem from the absence of a system in the child's spontaneous concepts — a consequence of undeveloped relations of generality. For example, to be disturbed by a contradiction, the child would have to view the contradictory statements in the light of some general principle, i.e., within a system. But when a child in Piaget's experiments says of one object that it dissolved in water because it was small, and of another that it dissolved because it was big, he merely makes empirical statements of facts which follow the logic of perceptions. No generalization of the kind "Smallness leads to dissolution" is present in his mind, and hence the two statements are not felt to be contradictory. It is this lack of distance from the immediate experience — and not syncretism viewed as a compromise between the logic of dreams and reality — that accounts for the peculiarities of child thought. Therefore these peculiarities do not appear in the child's scientific concepts, which from their very inception carry within them relationships of generality, i.e., some rudiments of a system. The formal discipline of scientific concepts gradually transforms the structure of the child's spontaneous concepts and helps organize them into a system; this furthers the child's ascent to higher developmental levels.

Our disagreement with Piaget centers on one point only, but an important point. He assumes that development and instruction are entirely separate, incommensurate processes, that the function of instruction is merely to introduce adult ways of thinking, which conflict with the child's own and eventually supplant them. Studying child thought apart from the influence of instruction, as Piaget did, excludes a very important source of change and bars the researcher from posing the question of the interaction of development and instruction peculiar to each age level. Our own approach focuses on this interaction. Having found many complex inner ties between spontaneous and scientific concepts, we hope that future comparative investigations will further clarify their interdependence, and we anticipate an extension of the study of development and instruction to lower age levels. Instruction, after all, does not begin in school. A future investigator may well find that the child's spontaneous concepts are a product of preschool instruction, just as scientific concepts are a product of school instruction.

V

Apart from theoretical conclusions, our comparative study of scientific and everyday concepts yielded some important methodological results. The methods we worked out for use in this study permit us to bridge the gap between the investigations of experimental and of real concepts. The information gathered on the mental processes of the schoolchild studying social science, schematic and rudimentary as it is, has suggested some possible improvements in the teaching of that subject.

In retrospect, we are aware of some omissions and of some methodological defects, perhaps inevitable in a first approach to a new field. We did not study experimentally and in detail the nature of the schoolchild's everyday concepts. This leaves us without the data needed to describe the total course of psychological development during school age; hence, our criticism of Piaget's basic theses is insufficiently buttressed by reliable, systematically obtained facts.

The study of scientific concepts was conducted in one category only — social science concepts — and the particular concepts selected for study do not form or suggest a system inherent in the logic of the subject. While we learned a good deal about the development of scientific compared with spontaneous concepts, we learned little about the regularities specific to the development of sociological concepts as such. Future studies should include concepts from various fields of school instruction, each set matched against a set of everyday concepts drawn from a similar area of experience.

Last but not least, the conceptual structures that we studied were not sufficiently differentiated. For example, in using sentence fragments ending in *because,* we did not separate the various types of causal relations (empirical, psychological, logical) as Piaget did in his studies. Had we done that, we might have been able to make a finer differentiation between the test performance of schoolchildren of different ages.

These very flaws, however, help in mapping the course of future investigations. The present study is merely a first, very modest step in exploring a new and highly promising area in the psychology of child thought.

7

Thought and Word

I have forgotten the word I intended to say, and my thought, unembodied, returns to the realm of shadows.[*]

I

WE BEGAN our study with an attempt to discover the relation between thought and speech at the earliest stages of phylogenetic and ontogenetic development. We found no specific interdependence between the genetic roots of thought and of word. It became plain that the inner relationship we were looking for was not a prerequisite for, but rather a product of, the historical development of human consciousness.

In animals, even in anthropoids whose speech is phonetically like human speech and whose intellect is akin to man's, speech and thinking are not interrelated. A prelinguistic period in thought and a preintellectual period in speech undoubtedly exist also in the development of the child. Thought and word are not connected by a primary bond. A connection originates, changes, and grows in the course of the evolution of thinking and speech.

It would be wrong, however, to regard thought and speech as two unrelated processes, either parallel or crossing at certain points and mechanically influencing each other. The absence of a primary bond does not mean that a connection between them

[*] From a poem by O. Mandelstam.

can be formed only in a mechanical way. The futility of most of
the earlier investigations was largely due to the assumption that
thought and word were isolated, independent elements, and
verbal thought the fruit of their external union.

The method of analysis based on this conception was bound
to fail. It sought to explain the properties of verbal thought by
breaking it up into its component elements, thought and word,
neither of which, taken separately, possesses the properties of
the whole. This method is not true analysis helpful in solving
concrete problems. It leads, rather, to generalization. We compared it to the analysis of water into hydrogen and oxygen —
which can result only in findings applicable to all water existing
in nature, from the Pacific Ocean to a raindrop. Similarly, the
statement that verbal thought is composed of intellectual processes and speech functions proper applies to all verbal thought
and all its manifestations and explains none of the specific problems facing the student of verbal thought.

We tried a new approach to the subject and replaced analysis
into elements by analysis into *units,* each of which retains in
simple form all the properties of the whole. We found this unit
of verbal thought in *word meaning.*

The meaning of a word represents such a close amalgam of
thought and language that it is hard to tell whether it is a phenomenon of speech or a phenomenon of thought. A word without meaning is an empty sound; meaning, therefore, is a criterion of "word," its indispensable component. It would seem,
then, that it may be regarded as a phenomenon of speech. But
from the point of view of psychology, the meaning of every
word is a generalization or a concept. And since generalizations
and concepts are undeniably acts of thought, we may regard
meaning as a phenomenon of thinking. It does not follow, however, that meaning formally belongs in two different spheres of
psychic life. Word meaning is a phenomenon of thought only
in so far as thought is embodied in speech, and of speech only
in so far as speech is connected with thought and illumined by
it. It is a phenomenon of verbal thought, or meaningful speech
— a union of word and thought.

Our experimental investigations fully confirm this basic thesis. They not only proved that concrete study of the development of verbal thought is made possible by the use of word meaning as the analytical unit but they also led to a further thesis, which we consider the major result of our study and which issues directly from the first: the thesis that word meanings develop. This insight must replace the postulate of the immutability of word meanings.

From the point of view of the old schools of psychology, the bond between word and meaning is an associative bond, established through the repeated simultaneous perception of a certain sound and a certain object. A word calls to mind its content as the overcoat of a friend reminds us of that friend, or a house of its inhabitants. The association between word and meaning may grow stronger or weaker, be enriched by linkage with other objects of a similar kind, spread over a wider field, or become more limited, i.e., it may undergo quantitative and external changes, but it cannot change its psychological nature. To do that, it would have to cease being an association. From that point of view, any development in word meanings is inexplicable and impossible — an implication which handicapped linguistics as well as psychology. Once having committed itself to the association theory, semantics persisted in treating word meaning as an association between a word's sound and its content. All words, from the most concrete to the most abstract, appeared to be formed in the same manner in regard to meaning, and to contain nothing peculiar to speech as such; a word made us think of its meaning just as any object might remind us of another. It is hardly surprising that semantics did not even pose the larger question of the development of word meanings. Development was reduced to changes in the associative connections between single words and single objects: A word might denote at first one object and then become associated with another, just as an overcoat, having changed owners, might remind us first of one person and later of another. Linguistics did not realize that in the historical evolution of language the very structure of meaning and its psychological nature also change. From primitive generalizations, verbal thought rises to the most abstract concepts. It is not merely the content of a word that changes, but the way in which reality is generalized and reflected in a word.

Equally inadequate is the association theory in explaining the development of word meanings in childhood. Here, too, it can account only for the purely external, quantitative changes in the bonds uniting word and meaning, for their enrichment and strengthening, but not for the fundamental structural and psychological changes that can and do occur in the development of language in children.

Oddly enough, the fact that associationism in general had been abandoned for some time did not seem to affect the interpretation of word and meaning. The Wuerzburg school, whose main object was to prove the impossibility of reducing thinking to a mere play of associations and to demonstrate the existence of specific laws governing the flow of thought, did not revise the association theory of word and meaning, or even recognize the need for such a revision. It freed thought from the fetters of sensation and imagery and from the laws of association, and turned it into a purely spiritual act. By so doing, it went back to the prescientific concepts of St. Augustine and Descartes and finally reached extreme subjective idealism. The psychology of thought was moving toward the ideas of Plato. Speech, at the same time, was left at the mercy of association. Even after the work of the Wuerzburg school, the connection between a word and its meaning was still considered a simple associative bond. The word was seen as the external concomitant of thought, its attire only, having no influence on its inner life. Thought and speech had never been as widely separated as during the Wuerzburg period. The overthrow of the association theory in the field of thought actually increased its sway in the field of speech.

The work of other psychologists further reinforced this trend. Selz continued to investigate thought without considering its relation to speech and came to the conclusion that man's productive thinking and the mental operations of chimpanzees were identical in nature — so completely did he ignore the influence of words on thought.

Even Ach, who made a special study of word meaning and who tried to overcome associationism in his theory of concepts, did not go beyond assuming the presence of "determining tendencies" operative, along with associations, in the process of concept formation. Hence, the conclusions he reached did not change the old understanding of word meaning. By identifying concept with meaning, he did not allow for development and changes in concepts. Once established, the meaning of a word was set forever; its development was completed. The same principles were taught by the very psychologists Ach attacked. To both sides, the starting point was also the end of the development of a concept; the disagreement concerned only the way in which the formation of word meanings began.

In Gestalt psychology, the situation was not very different. This school was more consistent than others in trying to surmount the general principle of associationism. Not satisfied with a partial solution of the problem, it tried to liberate thinking *and* speech from the rule of association and to put both under the laws of structure formation. Surprisingly, even this most progressive of modern psychological schools made no progress in the theory of thought and speech.

For one thing, it retained the complete separation of these two functions. In the light of Gestalt psychology, the relationship between thought and word appears as a simple analogy, a reduction of both to a common structural denominator. The formation of the first meaningful words of a child is seen as similar to the intellectual operations of chimpanzees in Koehler's experiments. Words enter into the structure of things and acquire a certain functional meaning, in much the same way as the stick, to the chimpanzee, becomes part of the structure of obtaining the fruit and acquires the functional meaning of tool. The connection between word and meaning is no longer regarded as a matter of simple association but as a matter of structure. That seems like a step forward. But if we look more closely at the new approach, it is easy to see that the step forward is an illusion and that we are still standing in the same place. The principle of structure is applied to all relations between things in the same sweeping, undifferentiated way as the principle of association was before it. It remains impossible to deal with the specific relations between word and meaning.

They are from the outset accepted as identical in principle with any and all other relations between things. All cats are as gray in the dusk of Gestalt psychology as in the earlier fogs of universal associationism.

While Ach sought to overcome associationism with the "determining tendency," Gestalt psychology combated it with the principle of structure — retaining, however, the two fundamental errors of the older theory: the assumption of the identical nature of all connections and the assumption that word meanings do not change. The old and the new psychology both assume that the development of a word's meaning is finished as soon as it emerges. The new trends in psychology brought progress in all branches except in the study of thought and speech. Here the new principles resemble the old ones like twins.

If Gestalt psychology is at a standstill in the field of speech, it has made a big step backward in the field of thought. The Wuerzburg school at least recognized that thought had laws of its own. Gestalt psychology denies their existence. By reducing to a common structural denominator the perceptions of domestic fowl, the mental operations of chimpanzees, the first meaningful words of the child, and the conceptual thinking of the adult, it obliterates every distinction between the most elementary perception and the highest forms of thought.

This critical survey may be summed up as follows: All the psychological schools and trends overlook the cardinal point that every thought is a generalization; and they all study word and meaning without any reference to development. As long as these two conditions persist in the successive trends, there cannot be much difference in the treatment of the problem.

II

The discovery that word meanings evolve leads the study of thought and speech out of a blind alley. Word meanings are dynamic rather than static formations. They change as the child develops; they change also with the various ways in which thought functions.

If word meanings change in their inner nature, then the relation of thought to word also changes. To understand the dynamics of that relationship, we must supplement the genetic approach of our main study by functional analysis and examine the role of word meaning in the process of thought.

Let us consider the process of verbal thinking from the first dim stirring of a thought to its formulation. What we want to show now is not how meanings develop over long periods of time but the way they function in the live process of verbal thought. On the basis of such a functional analysis, we shall be able to show also that each stage in the development of word meaning has its own particular relationship between thought and speech. Since functional problems are most readily solved by examining the highest form of a given activity, we shall, for a while, put aside the problem of development and consider the relations between thought and word in the mature mind.

The leading idea in the following discussion can be reduced to this formula: The relation of thought to word is not a thing but a process, a continual movement back and forth from thought to word and from word to thought. In that process the relation of thought to word undergoes changes which themselves may be regarded as development in the functional sense. Thought is not merely expressed in words; it comes into existence through them. Every thought tends to connect something with something else, to establish a relationship between things. Every thought moves, grows and develops, fulfills a function, solves a problem. This flow of thought occurs as an inner movement through a series of planes. An analysis of the interaction of thought and word must begin with an investigation of the different phases and planes a thought traverses before it is embodied in words.

The first thing such a study reveals is the need to distinguish between two planes of speech. Both the inner, meaningful, semantic aspect of speech and the external, phonetic aspect, though forming a true unity, have their own laws of movement. The unity of speech is a complex, not a homogeneous, unity. A number of facts in the linguistic development of the child indicate independent movement in the phonetic and the semantic spheres. We shall point out two of the most important of these facts.

In mastering external speech, the child starts from one word, then connects two or three words; a little later, he advances from simple sentences to more complicated ones, and finally to coherent speech made up of series of such sentences; in other words, he proceeds from a part to the whole. In regard to meaning, on the other hand, the first word of the child is a whole sentence. Semantically, the child starts from the whole, from a meaningful complex, and only later begins to master the separate semantic units, the meanings of words, and to divide his formerly undifferentiated thought into those units. The external and the semantic aspects of speech develop in opposite directions — one from the particular to the whole, from word to sentence, and the other from the whole to the particular, from sentence to word.

This in itself suffices to show how important it is to distinguish between the vocal and the semantic aspects of speech. Since they move in reverse directions, their development does not coincide, but that does not mean that they are independent of each other. On the contrary, their difference is the first stage of a close union. In fact, our example reveals their inner relatedness as clearly as it does their distinction. A child's thought, precisely because it is born as a dim, amorphous whole, must find expression in a single word. As his thought becomes more differentiated, the child is less apt to express it in single words but constructs a composite whole. Conversely, progress in speech to the differentiated whole of a sentence helps the child's thoughts to progress from a homogeneous whole to well-defined parts. Thought and word are not cut from one pattern. In a sense, there are more differences than likenesses between them. The structure of speech does not simply mirror the structure of thought; that is why words cannot be put on by thought like a ready-made garment. Thought undergoes many changes as it turns into speech. It does not merely find expression in speech; it finds its reality and form. The semantic and the phonetic developmental processes are essentially one, precisely because of their reverse directions.

The second, equally important fact emerges at a later period of development. Piaget demonstrated that the child uses subordinate clauses with *because, although*, etc., long before he grasps the structures of meaning corresponding to these syntactic forms. Grammar precedes logic. Here, too, as in our previous example, the discrepancy does not exclude union but is, in fact, necessary for union.

In adults the divergence between the semantic and the phonetic aspects of speech is even more striking. Modern, psychologically oriented linguistics is familiar with this phenomenon, especially in regard to grammatical and psychological subject and predicate. For example, in the sentence "The clock fell," emphasis and meaning may change in different situations. Suppose I notice that the clock has stopped and ask how this happened. The answer is, "The clock fell." Grammatical and psychological subject coincide: "The clock" is the first idea in my consciousness; "fell" is what is said about the clock. But if I hear a crash in the next room and inquire what happened, and get the same answer, subject and predicate are psychologically reversed. I knew something had fallen — that is what we are talking about. "The clock" completes the idea. The sentence could be changed to: "What has fallen is the clock"; then the grammatical and the psychological subject would coincide. In the prologue to his play *Duke Ernst von Schwaben,* Uhland says: "Grim scenes will pass before you." Psychologically, "will pass" is the subject. The spectator knows he will see events unfold; the additional idea, the predicate, is "grim scenes." Uhland meant, "What will pass before your eyes is a tragedy." Any part of a sentence may become the psychological predicate, the carrier of topical emphasis; on the other hand, entirely different meanings may lie hidden behind one grammatical structure. Accord between syntactical and psychological organization is not as prevalent as we tend to assume — rather, it is a requirement that is seldom met. Not only subject and predicate, but grammatical gender, number, case, tense, degree, etc., have their psychological doubles. A spontaneous utterance, wrong from the point of view of grammar, may have charm and aesthetic value. Absolute correctness is achieved only beyond natural language, in mathematics. Our daily speech continually fluctuates between the ideals of mathematical and of imaginative harmony.

We shall illustrate the interdependence of the semantic and the grammatical aspects of language by citing two examples which show that changes in formal structure can entail far-reaching changes in meaning.*

In translating the fable "La Cigale et la Fourmi," Krylov substituted a dragonfly for La Fontaine's grasshopper. In French *grasshopper* is feminine and therefore well suited to symbolize a lighthearted, carefree attitude. The nuance would be lost in a literal translation, since in Russian *grasshopper* is masculine. When he settled for *dragonfly*, which is feminine in Russian, Krylov disregarded the literal meaning in favor of the grammatical form required to render La Fontaine's thought.

Tjutchev did the same in his translation of Heine's poem about a fir and a palm. In German *fir* is masculine and *palm* feminine, and the poem suggests the love of a man for a woman. In Russian, both trees are feminine. To retain the implication, Tjutchev replaced the fir by a masculine cedar. Lermontov, in his more literal translation of the same poem, deprived it of these poetic overtones and gave it an essentially different meaning, more abstract and generalized. One grammatical detail may, on occasion, change the whole purport of what is said.

Behind words, there is the independent grammar of thought, the syntax of word meanings. The simplest utterance, far from reflecting a constant, rigid correspondence between sound and meaning, is really a process. Verbal expressions cannot emerge fully formed but must develop gradually. This complex process of transition from meaning to sound must itself be developed and perfected. The child must learn to distinguish between semantics and phonetics and understand the nature of the difference. At first he uses verbal forms and meanings without being conscious of them as separate. The word, to the child, is an integral part of the object it denotes. Such a conception

---

* Vygotsky's examples lose some of their impact in English because English grammar does not distinguish between genders. Some explanations have been added to make the point. — *Editor.*

seems to be characteristic of primitive linguistic consciousness. We all know the old story about the rustic who said he wasn't surprised that savants with all their instruments could figure out the size of stars and their course — what baffled him was how they found out their names. Simple experiments show that preschool children "explain" the names of objects by their attributes. According to them, an animal is called "cow" because it has horns, "calf" because its horns are still small, "dog" because it is small and has no horns; an object is called "car" because it is not an animal. When asked whether one could interchange the names of objects, for instance call a cow "ink," and ink "cow," children will answer no, "because ink is used for writing, and the cow gives milk." An exchange of names would mean an exchange of characteristic features, so inseparable is the connection between them in the child's mind. In one experiment, the children were told that in a game a dog would be called "cow." Here is a typical sample of questions and answers:

"Does a cow have horns?"

"Yes."

"But don't you remember that the cow is really a dog? Come now, does a dog have horns?"

"Sure, if it is a cow, if it's called cow, it has horns. That kind of dog has got to have little horns."

We can see how difficult it is for children to separate the name of an object from its attributes, which cling to the name when it is transferred like possessions following their owner.

The fusion of the two planes of speech, semantic and vocal, begins to break down as the child grows older, and the distance between them gradually increases. Each stage in the development of word meanings has its own specific interrelation of the two planes. A child's ability to communicate through language is directly related to the differentiation of word meanings in his speech and consciousness.

To understand this, we must remember a basic characteristic of the structure of word meanings. In the semantic structure of a word, we distinguish between referent and meaning; correspondingly, we distinguish a word's nominative from its significative function. When we compare these structural and functional relations at the earliest, middle, and advanced stages of development, we find the following genetic regularity: In the beginning, only the nominative function exists; and semantically, only the objective reference; signification independent of naming, and meaning independent of reference, appear later and develop along the paths we have attempted to trace and describe.

Only when this development is completed does the child become fully able to formulate his own thought and to understand the speech of others. Until then, his usage of words coincides with that of adults in its objective reference but not in its meaning.

III

We must probe still deeper and explore the plane of inner speech lying beyond the semantic plane. We shall discuss here some of the data of the special investigation we have made of it. The relationship of thought and word cannot be understood in all its complexity without a clear understanding of the psychological nature of inner speech. Yet, of all the problems connected with thought and language, this is perhaps the most complicated, beset as it is with terminological and other misunderstandings.

The term *inner speech,* or *endophasy,* has been applied to various phenomena, and authors argue about different things that they call by the same name. Originally, inner speech seems to have been understood as verbal memory. An example would be the silent recital of a poem known by heart. In that case, inner speech differs from vocal speech only as the idea or image of an object differs from the real object. It was in this sense that inner speech was understood by the French authors who tried to find out how words were reproduced in memory — whether as auditory, visual, motor, or synthetic images. We shall see that word memory is indeed one of the constituent elements of inner speech but not all of it.

In a second interpretation, inner speech is seen as truncated external speech — as "speech minus sound" (Mueller) or "subvocal speech" (Watson). Bekhterev defined it as a speech reflex inhibited in its motor part. Such an explanation is by no means sufficient. Silent "pronouncing" of words is not equivalent to the total process of inner speech.

The third definition is, on the contrary, too broad. To Goldstein [*12, 13*], the term covers everything that precedes the motor act of speaking, including Wundt's "motives of speech" and the indefinable, nonsensory and nonmotor specific speech experience — i.e., the whole interior aspect of any speech activity. It is hard to accept the equation of inner speech with an inarticulate inner experience in which the separate identifiable structural planes are dissolved without trace. This central experience is common to all linguistic activity, and for this reason alone Goldstein's interpretation does not fit that specific, unique function that alone deserves the name of inner speech. Logically developed, Goldstein's view must lead to the thesis that inner speech is not speech at all but rather an intellectual and affective-volitional activity, since it includes the motives of speech and the thought that is expressed in words.

To get a true picture of inner speech, one must start from the assumption that it is a specific formation, with its own laws and complex relations to the other forms of speech activity. Before we can study its relation to thought, on the one hand, and to speech, on the other, we must determine its special characteristics and function.

Inner speech is speech for oneself; external speech is for others. It would indeed be surprising if such a basic difference in function did not affect the structure of the two kinds of speech. Absence of vocalization per se is only a consequence of the specific nature of inner speech, which is neither an antecedent of external speech nor its reproduction in memory but is, in a sense, the opposite of external speech. The latter is the turning of thought into words, its materialization and objectification. With inner speech, the process is reversed: Speech turns into inward thought. Consequently, their structures must differ.

The area of inner speech is one of the most difficult to investigate. It remained almost inaccessible to experiments until ways were found to apply the genetic method of experimentation. Piaget was the first to pay attention to the child's egocentric speech and to see its theoretical significance, but he remained blind to the most important trait of egocentric speech — its genetic connection with inner speech — and this warped his interpretation of its function and structure. We made that relationship the central problem of our study and thus were able to investigate the nature of inner speech with unusual completeness. A number of considerations and observations led us to conclude that egocentric speech is a stage of development preceding inner speech: Both fulfill intellectual functions; their structures are similar; egocentric speech disappears at school age, when inner speech begins to develop. From all this we infer that one changes into the other.

If this transformation does take place, then egocentric speech provides the key to the study of inner speech. One advantage of approaching inner speech through egocentric speech is its accessibility to experimentation and observation. It is still vocalized, audible speech, i.e., external in its mode of expression, but at the same time inner speech in function and structure. To study an internal process it is necessary to externalize it experimentally, by connecting it with some outer activity; only then is objective functional analysis possible. Egocentric speech is, in fact, a natural experiment of this type.

This method has another great advantage: Since egocentric speech can be studied at the time when some of its characteristics are waning and new ones forming, we are able to judge which traits are essential to inner speech and which are only temporary, and thus to determine the goal of this movement from egocentric to inner speech — i.e., the nature of inner speech.

Before we go on to the results obtained by this method, we shall briefly discuss the nature of egocentric speech, stressing the differences between our theory and Piaget's. Piaget contends that the child's egocentric speech is a direct expression of the egocentrism of his thought, which in turn is a compromise between the primary autism of his thinking and its gradual socialization. As the child grows older, autism recedes and socialization progresses, leading to the waning of egocentrism in his thinking and speech.

In Piaget's conception, the child in his egocentric speech does not adapt himself to the thinking of adults. His thought remains entirely egocentric; this makes his talk incomprehensible to others. Egocentric speech has no function in the child's realistic thinking or activity — it merely accompanies them. And since it is an expression of egocentric thought, it disappears together with the child's egocentrism. From its climax at the beginning of the child's development, egocentric speech drops to zero on the threshold of school age. Its history is one of involution rather than evolution. It has no future.

In our conception, egocentric speech is a phenomenon of the transition from interpsychic to intrapsychic functioning, i.e., from the social, collective activity of the child to his more individualized activity — a pattern of development common to all the higher psychological functions. Speech for oneself originates through differentiation from speech for others. Since the main course of the child's development is one of gradual individualization, this tendency is reflected in the function and structure of his speech.

Our experimental results indicate that the function of egocentric speech is similar to that of inner speech: It does not merely accompany the child's activity; it serves mental orientation, conscious understanding; it helps in overcoming difficulties; it is speech for oneself, intimately and usefully connected with the child's thinking. Its fate is very different from that described by Piaget. Egocentric speech develops along a rising, not a declining, curve; it goes through an evolution, not an involution. In the end, it becomes inner speech.

Our hypothesis has several advantages over Piaget's: It explains the function and development of egocentric speech and, in particular, its sudden increase when the child faces difficulties which demand consciousness and reflection — a fact uncovered by our experiments and which Piaget's theory cannot explain. But the greatest advantage of our theory is that it supplies a satisfying answer to a paradoxical situation described by Piaget himself. To Piaget, the quantitative drop in egocentric speech as the child grows older means the withering of that form of speech. If that were so, its structural peculiarities might also be expected to decline; it is hard to believe that the process would affect only its quantity, and not its inner structure. The child's thought becomes infinitely less egocentric between the ages of three and seven. If the characteristics of egocentric speech that make it incomprehensible to others are indeed rooted in egocentrism, they should become less apparent as that form of speech becomes less frequent; egocentric speech should approach social speech and become more and more intelligible. Yet what are the facts? Is the talk of a three-year-old harder to follow than that of a seven-year-old? Our investigation established that the traits of egocentric speech which make for inscrutability are at their lowest point at three and at their peak at seven. They develop in a reverse direction to the frequency of egocentric speech. While the latter keeps falling and reaches zero at school age, the structural characteristics become more and more pronounced.

This throws a new light on the quantitative decrease in egocentric speech, which is the cornerstone of Piaget's thesis.

What does this decrease mean? The structural peculiarities of speech for oneself and its differentiation from external speech increase with age. What is it then that diminishes? Only one of its aspects: vocalization. Does this mean that egocentric speech as a whole is dying out? We believe that it does not, for how then could we explain the growth of the functional and structural traits of egocentric speech? On the other hand, their growth is perfectly compatible with the decrease of vocalization — indeed, clarifies its meaning. Its rapid dwindling and the equally rapid growth of the other characteristics are contradictory in appearance only.

To explain this, let us start from an undeniable, experimentally established fact. The structural and functional qualities of egocentric speech become more marked as the child develops. At three, the difference between egocentric and social speech equals zero; at seven, we have speech that in structure and function is totally unlike social speech. A differentiation of the two speech functions has taken place. This is a fact — and facts are notoriously hard to refute.

Once we accept this, everything else falls into place. If the developing structural and functional peculiarities of egocentric speech progressively isolate it from external speech, then its vocal aspect must fade away; and this is exactly what happens between three and seven years. With the progressive isolation of speech for oneself, its vocalization becomes unnecessary and meaningless and, because of its growing structural peculiarities, also impossible. Speech for oneself cannot find expression in external speech. The more independent and autonomous egocentric speech becomes, the poorer it grows in its external manifestations. In the end it separates itself entirely from speech for others, ceases to be vocalized, and thus appears to die out.

But this is only an illusion. To interpret the sinking coefficient of egocentric speech as a sign that this kind of speech is dying out is like saying that the child stops counting when he ceases to use his fingers and starts adding in his head. In reality, behind the symptoms of dissolution lies a progressive development, the birth of a new speech form.

The decreasing vocalization of egocentric speech denotes a developing abstraction from sound, the child's new faculty to "think words" instead of pronouncing them. This is the positive meaning of the sinking coefficient of egocentric speech. The downward curve indicates development toward inner speech.

We can see that all the known facts about the functional, structural, and genetic characteristics of egocentric speech point to one thing: It develops in the direction of inner speech. Its developmental history can be understood only as a gradual unfolding of the traits of inner speech.

We believe that this corroborates our hypothesis about the origin and nature of egocentric speech. To turn our hypothesis into a certainty, we must devise an experiment capable of showing which of the two interpretations is correct. What are the data for this critical experiment?

Let us restate the theories between which we must decide. Piaget believes that egocentric speech stems from the insufficient socialization of speech and that its only development is decrease and eventual death. Its culmination lies in the past. Inner speech is something new brought in from the outside along with socialization. We believe that egocentric speech stems from the insufficient individualization of primary social speech. Its culmination lies in the future. It develops into inner speech.

To obtain evidence for one or the other view, we must place the child alternately in experimental situations encouraging social speech and in situations discouraging it, and see how these changes affect egocentric speech. We consider this an *experimentum crucis* for the following reasons.

If the child's egocentric talk results from the egocentrism of his thinking and its insufficient socialization, then any weakening of the social elements in the experimental setup, any factor contributing to the child's isolation from the group, must lead to a sudden increase in egocentric speech. But if the latter results from an insufficient differentiation of speech for oneself from speech for others, then the same changes must cause it to decrease.

We took as the starting point of our experiment three of Piaget's own observations: (1) Egocentric speech occurs only in the presence of other children engaged in the same activity, and not when the child is alone; i.e., it is a collective monologue. (2) The child is under the illusion that his egocentric talk, directed to nobody, is understood by those who surround him. (3) Egocentric speech has the character of external speech: It is not inaudible or whispered. These are certainly not chance peculiarities. From the child's own point of view, egocentric speech is not yet separated from social speech. It occurs under the subjective and objective conditions of social speech and may be considered a correlate of the insufficient isolation of the child's individual consciousness from the social whole.

In our first series of experiments [46, 47], we tried to destroy the illusion of being understood. After measuring the child's coefficient of egocentric speech in a situation similar to that of Piaget's experiments, we put him into a new situation: either with deaf-mute children or with children speaking a foreign language. In all other respects the setup remained the same. The coefficient of egocentric speech dropped to zero in the majority of cases, and in the rest to one-eighth of the previous figure, on the average. This proves that the illusion of being understood is not a mere epiphenomenon of egocentric speech but is functionally connected with it. Our results must seem paradoxical from the point of view of Piaget's theory: The weaker the child's contact is with the group — the less the social situation forces him to adjust his thoughts to others and to use social speech — the more freely should the egocentrism of his thinking and speech manifest itself. But from the point of view of our hypothesis, the meaning of these findings is clear: Egocentric speech, springing from the lack of differentiation of speech for oneself from speech for others, disappears when the feeling of being understood, essential for social speech, is absent.

In the second series of experiments, the variable factor was the possibility of collective monologue. Having measured the child's coefficient of egocentric speech in a situation permitting collective monologue, we put him into a situation excluding it — in a group of children who were strangers to him, or by himself at a separate table in a corner of the room; or he worked quite alone, even the experimenter leaving the room. The results of this series agreed with the first results. The exclusion of the group monologue caused a drop in the coefficient of egocentric speech, though not such a striking one as in the first case — seldom to zero and, on the average, to one-sixth of the original figure. The different methods of precluding collective monologue were not equally effective in reducing the coefficient of egocentric speech. The trend, however, was obvious in all the variations of the experiment. The exclusion of the collective factor, instead of giving full freedom to egocentric speech, depressed it. Our hypothesis was once more confirmed.

In the third series of experiments, the variable factor was the vocal quality of egocentric speech. Just outside the laboratory where the experiment was in progress, an orchestra played so loudly, or so much noise was made, that it drowned out not only the voices of others but the child's own; in a variant of the experiment, the child was expressly forbidden to talk loudly and allowed to talk only in whispers. Once again the coefficient of egocentric speech went down, the relation to the original figure being 5:1. Again the different methods were not equally effective, but the basic trend was invariably present.

The purpose of all three series of experiments was to eliminate those characteristics of egocentric speech which bring it close to social speech. We found that this always led to the dwindling of egocentric speech. It is logical, then, to assume that egocentric speech is a form developing out of social speech and not yet separated from it in its manifestation, though already distinct in function and structure.

The disagreement between us and Piaget on this point will be made quite clear by the following example: I am sitting at my desk talking to a person who is behind me and whom I cannot see; he leaves the room without my noticing it, and I continue to talk, under the illusion that he listens and understands. Outwardly, I am talking with myself and for myself, but psychologically my speech is social. From the point of view of Piaget's theory, the opposite happens in the case of the child: His egocentric talk is for and with himself; it only has the appearance of social speech, just as my speech gave the false impression of being egocentric. From our point of view, the whole situation is much more complicated than that: Subjectively, the child's egocentric speech already has its own peculiar function — to that extent, it is independent from social speech; yet its independence is not complete because it is not felt as inner speech and is not distinguished by the child from speech for others. Objectively, also, it is different from social speech but again not entirely, because it functions only within social situations. Both subjectively and objectively, egocentric speech represents a transition from speech for others to speech for oneself. It already has the function of inner speech but remains similar to social speech in its expression.

The investigation of egocentric speech has paved the way to the understanding of inner speech, which we shall examine next.

IV

Our experiments convinced us that inner speech must be regarded, not as speech minus sound, but as an entirely separate speech function. Its main distinguishing trait is its peculiar syntax. Compared with external speech, inner speech appears disconnected and incomplete.

This is not a new observation. All the students of inner speech, even those who approached it from the behavioristic standpoint, noted this trait. The method of genetic analysis permits us to go beyond a mere description of it. We applied this method and found that as egocentric speech develops it shows a tendency toward an altogether specific form of abbreviation: namely, omitting the subject of a sentence and all words connected with it, while preserving the predicate. This tendency toward predication appears in all our experiments with such regularity that we must assume it to be the basic syntactic form of inner speech.

It may help us to understand this tendency if we recall certain situations in which external speech shows a similar structure. Pure predication occurs in external speech in two cases: either as an answer or when the subject of the sentence is known beforehand to all concerned. The answer to "Would you like a cup of tea?" is never "No, I don't want a cup of tea," but a simple "No." Obviously, such a sentence is possible only because its subject is tacitly understood by both parties. To "Has your brother read this book?" no one ever replies, "Yes, my brother has read this book." The answer is a short "Yes," or "Yes, he has." Now let us imagine that several people are waiting for a bus. No one will say, on seeing the bus approach, "The bus for which we are waiting is coming." The sentence is likely to be an abbreviated "Coming," or some such expression, because the subject is plain from the situation. Quite frequently, shortened sentences cause confusion. The listener may relate the sentence to a subject foremost in his own mind, not the one meant by the speaker. If the thoughts of two people coincide, perfect understanding can be achieved through the use of mere predicates, but if they are thinking about different things they are bound to misunderstand each other.

Very good examples of the condensation of external speech and its reduction to predicates are found in the novels of Tolstoy, who quite often dealt with the psychology of understanding: "No one heard clearly what he said, but Kitty understood him. She understood because her mind incessantly watched for his needs" [*Anna Karenina*, Pt. V, Ch. 18]. We might say that her thoughts, following the thoughts of the dying man, contained the subject to which his word, understood by no one else, referred. But perhaps the most striking example is the declaration of love between Kitty and Levin by means of initial letters:

"I have long wished to ask you something."

"Please do."

"This," he said, and wrote the initial letters: *W y a: i c n b, d y m t o n*. These letters meant: "When you answered: it can not be, did you mean then or never?" It seemed impossible that she would be able to understand the complicated sentence.

"I understand," she said, blushing.

"What word is that?" he asked, pointing to the *n* which stood for "never."

"The word is 'never,'" she said, "but that is not true." He quickly erased what he had written, handed her the chalk, and rose. She wrote: *I c n a o t.*

His face brightened suddenly: he had understood. It meant: "I could not answer otherwise then."

She wrote the initial letters: *s t y m f a f w h.* This meant: "So that you might forget and forgive what happened."

He seized the chalk with tense, trembling fingers, broke it, and wrote the initial letters of the following: "I have nothing to forget and forgive. I never ceased loving you."

"I understand," she whispered. He sat down and wrote a long sentence. She understood it all and, without asking him whether she was right, took the chalk and answered at once. For a long time he could not make out what she had written, and he kept looking up into her eyes. His mind was dazed with happiness. He was quite unable to fill in the words she had meant; but in her lovely, radiantly happy eyes he read all that he needed to know. And he wrote down three letters. Before he had finished writing, she was already reading under his hand, and she finished the sentence herself and wrote the answer, "yes." Everything had been said in their conversation: that she loved him, and would tell her father and mother that he would call in the morning. [*Anna Karenina*, Pt. IV, Ch. 13]

This example has an extraordinary psychological interest because, like the whole episode between Kitty and Levin, it was taken by Tolstoy from his own life. In just this way, Tolstoy told his future wife of his love for her. These examples show clearly that when the thoughts of the speakers are the same the role of speech is reduced to a minimum. Tolstoy points out elsewhere that between people who live in close psychological contact, such communication by means of abbreviated speech is the rule rather than the exception.

> Now Levin was used to expressing his thought fully without troubling to put it into exact words: He knew that his wife, in such moments filled with love, as this one, would understand what he wanted to say from a mere hint, and she did. [*Anna Karenina*, Pt. VI, Ch. 3]

A simplified syntax, condensation, and a greatly reduced number of words characterize the tendency to predication which appears in external speech when the partners know what is going on. In complete contrast to this kind of understanding are the comical mix-ups resulting from people's thoughts going in different directions. The confusion to which this may lead is well rendered in this little poem:

> Before the judge who's deaf two deaf men bow.
> One deaf man cries: "He led away my cow."
> "Beg pardon," says the other in reply,
> "That meadow was my father's land in days gone by."
> The judge decides: "For you to fight each other is a shame.
> Nor one nor t'other, but the girl's to blame."

Kitty's conversation with Levin and the judgment of the deaf are extreme cases, the two poles, in fact, of external speech. One exemplifies the mutual understanding that can be achieved through utterly abbreviated speech when the subject is the same in two minds; the other, the total misunderstanding, even with full speech, when people's thoughts wander in different directions. It is not only the deaf who cannot understand one another but any two people who give a different meaning to the same word or who hold divergent views. As Tolstoy noted, those who are accustomed to solitary, independent thinking do not easily grasp another's thought and are very partial to their own; but people in close contact apprehend one another's complicated meanings by "laconic and clear" communication in the fewest words.

V

Having examined abbreviation in external speech, we can now return enriched to the same phenomenon in inner speech, where it is not an exception but the rule. It will be instructive to compare abbreviation in oral, inner, and written speech. Communication in writing relies on the formal meanings of words and requires a much greater number of words than oral speech to convey the same idea. It is addressed to an absent person who rarely has in mind the same subject as the writer. Therefore it must be fully deployed; syntactic differentiation is at a maximum; and expressions are used that would seem unnatural in conversation. Griboedov's "He talks like writing" refers to the droll effect of elaborate constructions in daily speech.

The multifunctional nature of language, which has recently attracted the close attention of linguists, had already been pointed out by Humboldt in relation to poetry and prose — two forms very different in function and also in the means they use. Poetry, according to Humboldt, is inseparable from music, while prose depends entirely on language and is dominated by thought. Consequently, each has its own diction, grammar, and syntax. This is a conception of primary importance, although neither Humboldt nor those who further developed his thought fully realized its implications. They distinguished only between poetry and prose, and within the latter between the exchange of ideas and ordinary conversation, i.e., the mere exchange of news or conventional chatter. There are other important functional distinctions in speech. One of them is the distinction between dialogue and monologue. Written and inner speech represent the monologue; oral speech, in most cases, the dialogue.

Dialogue always presupposes in the partners sufficient knowledge of the subject to permit abbreviated speech and, under certain conditions, purely predicative sentences. It also presupposes that each person can see his partners, their facial expressions and gestures, and hear the tone of their voices. We have already discussed abbreviation and shall consider here only its auditory aspect, using a classical example from Dostoevski's *The Diary of a Writer* to show how much intonation helps the subtly differentiated understanding of a word's meaning.

Dostoevski relates a conversation of drunks which entirely consisted of one unprintable word:

> One Sunday night I happened to walk for some fifteen paces next to a group of six drunken young workmen, and I suddenly realized that all thoughts, feelings and even a whole chain of reasoning could be expressed by that one noun, which is moreover extremely short. One young fellow said it harshly and forcefully, to express his utter contempt for whatever it was they had all been talking about. Another answered with the same noun but in a quite different tone and sense — doubting that the negative attitude of the first one was warranted. A third suddenly became incensed against the first and roughly intruded on the conversation, excitedly shouting the same noun, this time as a curse and obscenity. Here the second fellow interfered again, angry at the third, the aggressor, and restraining him, in the sense of "Now why do you have to butt in, we were discussing things quietly and here you come and start swearing." And he told this whole thought in one word, the same venerable word, except that he also raised his hand and put it on the third fellow's shoulder. All at once a fourth, the youngest of the group, who had kept silent till then, probably having suddenly found a solution to the original difficulty which had started the argument, raised his hand in a transport of joy and shouted . . . Eureka, do you think? I have it? No, not eureka and not I have it; he repeated the same unprintable noun, one word, merely one word, but with ecstasy, in a shriek of delight — which was apparently too strong, because the sixth and the oldest, a glum-looking fellow, did not like it and cut the infantile joy of the other one short, addressing him in a sullen, exhortative bass and repeating . . . yes, still the same noun, forbidden in the presence of ladies but which this time clearly meant "What are you yelling yourself hoarse for?" So, without uttering a single other word, they repeated that one beloved word six times in a row, one after an-

other, and understood one another completely. [*The Diary of a Writer*, for 1873]

Inflection reveals the psychological context within which a word is to be understood. In Dostoevski's story, it was contemptuous negation in one case, doubt in another, anger in the third. When the context is as clear as in this example, it really becomes possible to convey all thoughts, feelings, and even a whole chain of reasoning by one word.

In written speech, as tone of voice and knowledge of subject are excluded, we are obliged to use many more words, and to use them more exactly. Written speech is the most elaborate form of speech.

Some linguists consider dialogue the natural form of oral speech, the one in which language fully reveals its nature, and monologue to a great extent artificial. Psychological investigation leaves no doubt that monologue is indeed the higher, more complicated form, and of later historical development. At present, however, we are interested in comparing them only in regard to the tendency toward abbreviation.

The speed of oral speech is unfavorable to a complicated process of formulation — it does not leave time for deliberation and choice. Dialogue implies immediate unpremeditated utterance. It consists of replies, repartee; it is a chain of reactions. Monologue, by comparison, is a complex formation; the linguistic elaboration can be attended to leisurely and consciously.

In written speech, lacking situational and expressive supports, communication must be achieved only through words and their combinations; this requires the speech activity to take complicated forms — hence the use of first drafts. The evolution from the draft to the final copy reflects our mental process. Planning has an important part in written speech, even when we do not actually write out a draft. Usually we say to ourselves what we are going to write; this is also a draft, though in thought only. As we tried to show in the preceding chapter, this mental draft is inner speech. Since inner speech functions as a draft not only in written but also in oral speech, we shall now compare both these forms with inner speech in respect to the tendency toward abbreviation and predication.

This tendency, never found in written speech and only sometimes in oral speech, arises in inner speech always. Predication is the natural form of inner speech; psychologically, it consists of predicates only. It is as much a law of inner speech to omit subjects as it is a law of written speech to contain both subjects and predicates.

The key to this experimentally established fact is the invariable, inevitable presence in inner speech of the factors that facilitate pure predication: We know what we are thinking about — i.e., we always know the subject and the situation. Psychological contact between partners in a conversation may establish a mutual perception leading to the understanding of abbreviated speech. In inner speech, the "mutual" perception is always there, in absolute form; therefore, a practically wordless "communication" of even the most complicated thoughts is the rule.

The predominance of predication is a product of development. In the beginning, egocentric speech is identical in structure with social speech, but in the process of its transformation into inner speech it gradually becomes less complete and coherent as it becomes governed by an almost entirely predicative syntax. Experiments show clearly how and why the new syntax takes hold. The child talks about the things he sees or hears or does at a given moment. As a result, he tends to leave out the subject and all words connected with it, condensing his speech more and more until only predicates are left. The more differentiated the specific function of egocentric speech becomes, the more pronounced are its syntactic peculiarities — simplification and predication. Hand in hand with this change goes decreasing vocalization. When we converse with ourselves, we need even fewer words than Kitty and Levin did. Inner speech is speech almost without words.

With syntax and sound reduced to a minimum, meaning is more than ever in the forefront. Inner speech works with semantics, not phonetics. The specific semantic structure of inner speech also contributes to abbreviation. The syntax of meanings in inner speech is no less original than its grammatical syntax. Our investigation established three main semantic peculiarities of inner speech.

The first and basic one is the preponderance of the *sense* of a word over its *meaning* — a distinction we owe to Paulhan. The sense of a word, according to him, is the sum of all the psychological events aroused in our consciousness by the word. It is a dynamic, fluid, complex whole, which has several zones of unequal stability. Meaning is only one of the zones of sense, the most stable and precise zone. A word acquires its sense from the context in which it appears; in different contexts, it changes its sense. Meaning remains stable throughout the changes of sense. The dictionary meaning of a word is no more than a stone in the edifice of sense, no more than a potentiality that finds diversified realization in speech.

The last words of the previously mentioned fable by Krylov, "The Dragonfly and the Ant," are a good illustration of the difference between sense and meaning. The words "Go and dance!" have a definite and constant meaning, but in the context of the fable they acquire a much broader intellectual and affective sense. They mean both "Enjoy yourself" and "Perish." This enrichment of words by the sense they gain from the context is the fundamental law of the dynamics of word meanings. A word in a context means both more and less than the same word in isolation: more, because it acquires new content; less, because its meaning is limited and narrowed by the context. The sense of a word, says Paulhan, is a complex, mobile, protean phenomenon; it changes in different minds and situations and is almost unlimited. A word derives its sense from the sentence, which in turn gets its sense from the paragraph, the paragraph from the book, the book from all the works of the author.

Paulhan rendered a further service to psychology by analyzing the relation between word and sense and showing that they are much more independent of each other than word and meaning. It has long been known that words can change their sense. Recently it was pointed out that sense can change words or, better, that ideas often change their names. Just as the sense of a word is connected with the whole word, and not with its single sounds, the sense of a sentence is connected with the whole sentence, and not with its individual words. Therefore, a word may sometimes be replaced by another without any change in sense. Words and sense are relatively independent of each other.

In inner speech, the predominance of sense over meaning, of sentence over word, and of context over sentence is the rule.

This leads us to the other semantic peculiarities of inner speech. Both concern word combination. One of them is rather like agglutination — a way of combining words fairly frequent in some languages and comparatively rare in others. German often forms one noun out of several words or phrases. In some primitive languages, such adhesion of words is a general rule. When several words are merged into one word, the new word not only expresses a rather complex idea but designates all the separate elements contained in that idea. Because the stress is always on the main root or idea, such languages are easy to understand. The egocentric speech of the child displays some analogous phenomena. As egocentric speech approaches inner speech, the child uses agglutination more and more as a way of forming compound words to express complex ideas.

The third basic semantic peculiarity of inner speech is the way in which senses of words combine and unite — a process governed by different laws from those governing combinations of meanings. When we observed this singular way of uniting words in egocentric speech, we called it "influx of sense." The senses of different words flow into one another — literally "influence" one another — so that the earlier ones are contained in, and modify, the later ones. Thus, a word that keeps recurring in a book or a poem sometimes absorbs all the variety of sense contained in it and becomes, in a way, equivalent to the work itself. The title of a literary work expresses its content and completes its sense to a much greater degree than does the name of a painting or of a piece of music. Titles like *Don Quixote,* *Hamlet,* and *Anna Karenina* illustrate this very clearly; the whole sense of a work is contained in one name. Another excellent example is Gogol's *Dead Souls.* Originally, the title referred to dead serfs whose names had not yet been removed from the official lists and who could still be bought and sold as if they were alive. It is in this sense that the words are used throughout the book, which is built up around this traffic in the dead. But through their intimate relationship with the work as a whole, these two words acquire a new significance, an infinitely broader sense. When we reach the end of the book, "Dead Souls" means to us not so much the defunct serfs as all the characters in the story who are alive physically but dead spiritually.

In inner speech, the phenomenon reaches its peak. A single word is so saturated with sense that many words would be required to explain it in external speech. No wonder that egocentric speech is incomprehensible to others. Watson says that inner speech would be incomprehensible even if it could be recorded. Its opaqueness is further increased by a related phenomenon which, incidentally, Tolstoy noted in external speech: In *Childhood, Adolescence, and Youth,* he describes how between people in close psychological contact words acquire special meanings understood only by the initiated. In inner speech, the same kind of idiom develops — the kind that is difficult to translate into the language of external speech.

With this we shall conclude our survey of the peculiarities of inner speech, which we first observed in our investigation of egocentric speech. In looking for comparisons in external speech, we found that the latter already contains, potentially at least, the traits typical of inner speech; predication, decrease of vocalization, preponderance of sense over meaning, agglutination, etc., appear under certain conditions also in external speech. This, we believe, is the best confirmation of our hypothesis that inner speech originates through the differentiation of egocentric speech from the child's primary social speech.

All our observations indicate that inner speech is an autonomous speech function. We can confidently regard it as a distinct plane of verbal thought. It is evident that the transition from inner to external speech is not a simple translation from one language into another. It cannot be achieved by merely vocalizing silent speech. It is a complex, dynamic process involving the transformation of the predicative, idiomatic structure of inner speech into syntactically articulated speech intelligible to others.

VI

We can now return to the definition of inner speech that we proposed before presenting our analysis. Inner speech is not the interior aspect of external speech — it is a function in itself. It still remains speech, i.e., thought connected with words. But while in external speech thought is embodied in words, in inner speech words die as they bring forth thought. Inner speech is to a large extent thinking in pure meanings. It is a dynamic, shifting, unstable thing, fluttering between word and thought, the two more or less stable, more or less firmly delineated components of verbal thought. Its true nature and place can be understood only after examining the next plane of verbal thought, the one still more inward than inner speech.

That plane is thought itself. As we have said, every thought creates a connection, fulfills a function, solves a problem. The flow of thought is not accompanied by a simultaneous unfolding of speech. The two processes are not identical, and there is no rigid correspondence between the units of thought and speech. This is especially obvious when a thought process miscarries — when, as Dostoevski put it, a thought "will not enter words." Thought has its own structure, and the transition from it to speech is no easy matter. The theater faced the problem of the thought behind the words before psychology did. In teaching his system of acting, Stanislavsky required the actors to uncover the "subtext" of their lines in a play. In Griboedov's comedy *Woe from Wit*, the hero, Chatsky, says to the heroine, who maintains that she has never stopped thinking of him, "Thrice blessed who believes. Believing warms the heart." Stanislavsky interpreted this as "Let us stop this talk"; but it could just as well be interpreted as "I do not believe you. You say it to comfort me," or as "Don't you see how you torment me? I wish I could believe you. That would be bliss." Every sentence that we say in real life has some kind of subtext, a thought hidden behind it. In the examples we gave earlier of the lack of coincidence between grammatical and psychological subject and predicate, we did not pursue our analysis to the end. Just as one sentence may express different thoughts, one thought may be expressed in different sentences. For instance,

"The clock fell," in answer to the question "Why did the clock stop?" could mean: "It is not my fault that the clock is out of order; it fell." The same thought, self-justification, could take the form of "It is not my habit to touch other people's things. I was just dusting here," or a number of others.

Thought, unlike speech, does not consist of separate units. When I wish to communicate the thought that today I saw a barefoot boy in a blue shirt running down the street, I do not see every item separately: the boy, the shirt, its blue color, his running, the absence of shoes. I conceive of all this in one thought, but I put it into separate words. A speaker often takes several minutes to disclose one thought. In his mind the whole thought is present at once, but in speech it has to be developed successively. A thought may be compared to a cloud shedding a shower of words. Precisely because thought does not have its automatic counterpart in words, the transition from thought to word leads through meaning. In our speech, there is always the hidden thought, the subtext. Because a direct transition from thought to word is impossible, there have always been laments about the inexpressibility of thought:

> How shall the heart express itself?
> How shall another understand?
>   [F. Tjutchev]

Direct communication between minds is impossible, not only physically but psychologically. Communication can be achieved only in a roundabout way. Thought must pass first through meanings and then through words.

We come now to the last step in our analysis of verbal thought. Thought itself is engendered by motivation, i.e., by our desires and needs, our interests and emotions. Behind every thought there is an affective-volitional tendency, which holds the answer to the last "why" in the analysis of thinking. A true and full understanding of another's thought is possible only when we understand its affective-volitional basis. We shall illustrate this by an example already used: the interpretation of parts in a play. Stanislavsky, in his instructions to actors, listed the motives behind the words of their parts. For example:

Text of the Play	*Parallel Motives*
SOPHYA:	
O, Chatsky, but I am glad you've come.	Tries to hide her confusion.
CHATSKY:	
You are glad, that's very nice; But gladness such as yours not easily one tells. It rather seems to me, all told, That making man and horse catch cold I've pleased myself and no one else.	Tries to make her feel guilty by teasing her. Aren't you ashamed of yourself! Tries to force her to be frank.
LIZA:	
There, sir, and if you'd stood on the same landing here Five minutes, no, not five ago You'd heard your name clear as clear. You say, Miss! Tell him it was so.	Tries to calm him. Tries to help Sophya in a difficult situation.
SOPHYA:	
And always so, no less, no more. No, as to that, I'm sure you can't reproach me.	Tries to reassure Chatsky. I am not guilty of anything!
CHATSKY:	
Well, let's suppose it's so. Thrice blessed who believes. Believing warms the heart.	Let us stop this conversation; etc.

[A. Griboedov, *Woe from Wit*, Act I]

To understand another's speech, it is not sufficient to understand his words — we must understand his thought. But even that is not enough — we must also know its motivation. No psychological analysis of an utterance is complete until that plane is reached.

We have come to the end of our analysis; let us survey its results. Verbal thought appeared as a complex, dynamic entity, and the relation of thought and word within it as a movement through a series of planes. Our analysis followed the process from the outermost to the innermost plane. In reality, the development of verbal thought takes the opposite course: from the motive which engenders a thought to the shaping of the thought, first in inner speech, then in meanings of words, and finally in words. It would be a mistake, however, to imagine that this is the only road from thought to word. The development may stop at any point in its complicated course; an infinite variety of movements to and fro, of ways still unknown to us, is possible. A study of these manifold variations lies beyond the scope of our present task.

Our investigation followed a rather unusual path. We wished to study the inner workings of thought and speech, hidden from direct observation. Meaning and the whole inward aspect of language, the side turned toward the person, not toward the outer world, have been so far an almost unknown territory. No matter how they were interpreted, the relations between thought and word were always considered constant, established forever. Our investigation has shown that they are, on the contrary, delicate, changeable relations between processes, which arise during the development of verbal thought. We did not intend to, and could not, exhaust the subject of verbal thought. We tried only to give a general conception of the infinite complexity of this dynamic structure — a conception starting from experimentally documented facts.

To association psychology, thought and word were united by external bonds, similar to the bonds between two nonsense syllables. Gestalt psychology introduced the concept of structural bonds but, like the older theory, did not account for the specific relations between thought and word. All the other theories grouped themselves around two poles — either the behaviorist concept of thought as speech minus sound or the idealistic view, held by the Wuerzburg school and Bergson, that thought could be "pure," unrelated to language, and that it was distorted by words. Tjutchev's "A thought once uttered is a lie" could well serve as an epigraph for the latter group. Whether inclining toward pure naturalism or extreme idealism, all these theories have one trait in common — their antihistorical bias. They study thought and speech without any reference to their developmental history.

Only a historical theory of inner speech can deal with this immense and complex problem. The relation between thought and word is a living process; thought is born through words. A word devoid of thought is a dead thing, and a thought unembodied in words remains a shadow. The connection between them, however, is not a preformed and constant one. It emerges in the course of development, and itself evolves. To the Biblical "In the beginning was the Word," Goethe makes Faust reply, "In the beginning was the deed." The intent here is to detract from the value of the word, but we can accept this version if we emphasize it differently: In the *beginning* was the deed. The word was not the beginning — action was there first; it is the end of development, crowning the deed.

We cannot close our survey without mentioning the perspectives that our investigation opens up. We studied the inward aspects of speech, which were as unknown to science as the other side of the moon. We showed that a generalized reflection of reality is the basic characteristic of words. This aspect of the word brings us to the threshold of a wider and deeper subject — the general problem of consciousness. Thought and language, which reflect reality in a way different from that of perception, are the key to the nature of human consciousness. Words play a central part not only in the development of thought but in the historical growth of consciousness as a whole. A word is a microcosm of human consciousness.

Bibliography

Bibliography

1. Ach, N., *Ueber die Begriffsbildung*. Bamberg, Buchner, 1921.
2. Arsen'eva, Zabolotnova, Kanushina, Chanturija, Èfes, Nejfec, and others. Unpublished theses of students of the Herzen Pedagogical Institute in Leningrad.
3. Bleuler, E., *Das autistisch-undisziplinierte Denken in der Medizin*. Berlin, J. Springer, 1927.
4. Borovskij, V., *Vvedenie v sravnitel'nuju psikhologiju [Introduction to Comparative Psychology]*. 1927.
5. Buehler, C., *Soziologische und psychologische Studien ueber das erste Lebensjahr*. Jena, G. Fischer, 1927.
6. Buehler, K., *Die geistige Entwicklung des Kindes*. Jena, G. Fischer, 1927.
7. ———, *Abriss der geistigen Entwicklung des Kindes*. Leipzig, Quelle & Meyer, 1928.
8. Delacroix, H., *Le langage et la pensée*. Paris, F. Alcan, 1924.
9. Engels, F., *Dialektik der Natur*. Moscow, Marx-Engels Verlag, 1935.
10. Frisch, K. v., "Ueber die 'Sprache' der Bienen." *Zool. Jb., Abt. Physiol.*, 40, 1923.
11. Gesell, A., *The Mental Growth of the Preschool Child*. New York, Macmillan, 1925.
12. Goldstein, K., "Ueber Aphasie." *Abh. aus d. Schw. Arch. f. Neurol. u. Psychiat.*, Heft 6, 1927.
13. ———, "Die pathologischen Tatsachen in ihrer Bedeutung fuer das Problem der Sprache." *Kongr. D. Ges. Psychol.*, 12, 1932.
14. Groos, K., *Das Seelenleben des Kindes*. Berlin, Reuther & Reichard, 1913.
15. Hanfmann, E., and Kasanin, J., "A Method for the Study of Concept Formation." *J. Psychol.*, 3, 1937.
16. ———, *Conceptual Thinking in Schizophrenia*. Nerv. and Ment. Dis. Monogr., 67, 1942.
17. Kafka, G., *Handbuch der vergleichenden Psychologie*, Bd. I, Abt. I. Muenchen, E. Reinhardt, 1922.
18. Koehler, W., *Intelligenzpruefungen an Menschenaffen*. Berlin, J. Springer, 1921.
19. ———, "Zur Psychologie des Schimpansen." *Psychol. Forsch.*, I, 1921.

20. Koffka, K., *Grundlagen der psychischen Entwicklung*. Osterwieck am Harz, A. W. Zickfeldt, 1925.

21. Kretschmer, E., *Medizinische Psychologie*. Leipzig, G. Thieme, 1926.

22. Kuelpe, O., "Sovremennaja psikhologija myshlenija" ["The Contemporary Psychology of Thinking"]. *Novye idei v filosofii*, 16, 1914.

23. Lemaitre, A., "Observations sur le langage intérieur des enfants." *Arch. de Psychol.*, 4, 1905.

24. Lenin, V., Konspekt knigi Gegelja *Nauka Logiki* [Outline of Hegel's book *The Science of Logic*]. Filosofskie tetradi, published by the CC of the CPSU(b), 1934.

25. Leontjew, A., and Luria, A., "Die psychologischen Anschauungen L. S. Wygotski's." *Ztschr. f. Psychol.*, 162, Heft 3-4, 1958.

26. Lévy-Bruhl, L., *Les fonctions mentales dans les sociétés inférieures*. Paris, F. Alcan, 1918.

27. Marx, K., *Das Kapital*, Bd. I. Hamburg, O. Meissner, 1914.

28. Meumann, E., "Die Entwicklung der ersten Wortbedeutungen beim Kinde." *Philos. Stud.*, 20, 1902.

29. Piaget, J., *Le langage et la pensée chez l'enfant*. Neuchâtel-Paris, Delachaux & Niestlé, 1923.

30. ———, *Le jugement et le raisonnement chez l'enfant*. Neuchâtel-Paris, Delachaux & Niestlé, 1924.

31. ———, *La représentation du monde chez l'enfant*. Paris, F. Alcan, 1926.

32. ———, *La causalité physique chez l'enfant*. Paris, F. Alcan, 1927.

33. ———, "Psychologie de l'enfant et l'enseignement de l'histoire." *Bulletin trimestriel de la Conférence Internationale pour l'enseignement de l'histoire*, 2, Paris 1933.

34. Plekhanov, G., *Ocherki po istorii materializma* [*Essays on the History of Materialism*]. 1922.

35. Rimat, F., *Intelligenzuntersuchungen anschliessend an die Ach'sche Suchmethode*. Goettingen, G. Calvoer, 1925.

36. Sakharov, L., "O metodakh issledovanija ponjatij" ["Methods of Investigating Concepts"]. *Psikhologija*, III, 1, 1930.

37. Shif, Zh., *Razvitie zhitejskikh i nauchnykh ponjatij* [*The Development of Scientific and Everyday Concepts*]. Moscow, Uchpedgiz, 1935.

38. Stern, C. u. W., *Die Kindersprache*. Leipzig, J. A. Barth, 1928.

39. Stern, W., *Person und Sache*, Bd. I. Leipzig, J. A. Barth, 1905.

40. ———, *Psychologie der fruehen Kindheit*. Leipzig, Quelle & Meyer, 1914.

41. Storch, A., *Das archaisch-primitive Erleben und Denken in der Schizophrenie*. Monogr. aus d. Gesamtgeb. d. Neurol. u. Psychiat., H. 32, 1922.

42. Thorndike, E., *The Mental Life of the Monkeys*. New York, Macmillan, 1901.

43. Tolstoy, L., *Pedagogicheskie stat'i* [*Pedagogical Essays*]. Kushnerev, 1903.

44. Usnadze, D., "Die Begriffsbildung im vorschulpflichtigen Alter." *Ztsch. f. angew. Psychol.*, 34, 1929.

45. ———, "Gruppenbildungsversuche bei vorschulpflichtigen Kindern." *Arch. ges. Psychol.,* 73, 1929.
46. Vygotsky, L., Luria, A., Leontiev, A., Levina, R., and others. Studies of egocentric speech. Unpublished.
47. Vygotsky, L., and Luria, A., "The Function and Fate of Egocentric Speech." *Proceed. of the Ninth Intern. Congr. of Psychol.* (New Haven, 1929). Princeton, Psychol. Rev. Company, 1930.
48. Vygotsky, L., Kotelova, Ju., Pashkovskaja, E. Experimental study of concept formation. Unpublished.
49. Vygotsky, L., "Eksperimental'noe issledovanie vysshikh processov povedenija" ["An Experimental Investigation of Higher Mental Processes"]. *Psikhonevrologicheskie nauki v S.S.S.R.,* Gosmedizdat, 1930.
50. ———, *Pedologija podrostka* [*Pedology of the Adolescent*]. Uchgiz, 1931.
51. ———, "Thought in Schizophrenia." *Arch. Neurol. Psychiat.,* 31, 1934.
52. ———, "Thought and Speech." *Psychiatry,* II, 1, 1939.
53. Volkelt, H., "Fortschritte der experimentellen Kinderpsychologie." *Kongr. f. exper. Psychol.,* 9, 1926. Jena, G. Fischer.
54. Watson, J., *Psychology from the Standpoint of a Behaviorist.* Philadelphia and London, G. B. Lippincott, 1919.
55. Werner, H., *Einfuehrung in die Entwicklungspsychologie.* Leipzig, J. A. Barth, 1926.
56. Wundt, W., *Voelkerpsychologie,* I. *Die Sprache.* Leipzig, W. Engelmann, 1900.
57. Yerkes, R. M., *The Mental Life of Monkeys and Apes.* Behav. Monogr., III, 1, 1916.
58. Yerkes, R. M., and Learned, B. W., *Chimpanzee Intelligence and Its Vocal Expression.* Baltimore, Williams & Wilkins, 1925.

Index

Index

229 608

Lightning Source UK Ltd.
Milton Keynes UK
UKOW051911270412

191634UK00001B/32/P

9 781614 272441